RETHINKING

FUELING
YOUR
COMPETITIVE
ADVANTAGE

RESILIENCE

Praise for *Rethinking Resilience*

"This book stopped me in my tracks—in the best way. *Rethinking Resilience* reframes how we show up as leaders under pressure. It's not about bouncing back, it's about moving forward with clarity, conviction, and connection. Every leader I know needs this lens—and this toolkit."

— Tia Newcomer, CEO, CaringBridge

"I devoured it! This book is a powerful and timely guide for navigating uncertainty with intention. The distinction between traditional/Reactive Resilience and Intentional Resilience completely reframed how I think about leadership. I never would have linked curiosity to resilience, but now I use it daily to open new thinking with my team. With personal stories, real-world coaching examples, and practical tools, this is a must-read for anyone looking to lead with clarity and strength in uncertain times."

— Krista Satterthwaite, Senior Vice President and General Manager, Mainstream Compute at Hewlett Packard Enterprise

"Every leader. Every company. Right now. This is the book you need to read to turn resilience into your sharpest strategic edge—and a blueprint for action."

— Nuala O'Connor, Senior Advisor, EqualAI, and Former SVP and Chief Counsel, Digital Citizenship, Walmart

"Tissa Richards masterfully redefines resilience not as our reaction to crisis but as a strategic design for continuous growth and competitive advantage. *Rethinking Resilience* provides a framework of forward-looking corporate leadership tools for our volatile world, where it isn't 'if' but 'when' you'll be stress-tested and operating amidst chaos."

— Andrew Borene, JD CISSP, Former Senior US Counterterrorism Official, Intelligence Officer, Combat Veteran, Board Member, and High-Risk/High-Payoff Initiatives Leader at Fortune 500 Firms

"This book flips resilience from a buzzword to a bottom-line advantage. No fluff, no pep talk—this is a blueprint. Sharp, actionable, and the clearest case I've seen for why resilience is your next strategic edge."

— Cali Ressler, Director, Talent and Organization Consulting, Global Employee Experience, Accenture

"If you're serious about thriving through change, not just surviving it, this is the guidebook you've been waiting for. It's not about bouncing back, it's about building forward. In *Rethinking Resilience*, you'll learn the mindset and the tools to embed resilience into the DNA of your leadership, teams, and organizations—a brilliant way to reframe resilience from a reactive necessity to a proactive, strategic advantage. Tissa Richards draws on her personal journey, compelling case studies, and insightful interviews with leaders across industries to introduce a powerful framework for building Intentional Resilience, one rooted in clarity, curiosity, conviction, and community."

— Joanna Kostecka, Vice President, Cloud Global Supply Chain Planning, Microsoft

"Read this book! It immediately captured my attention and imagination, the way *Lean In* did over a decade ago. It crisply and eloquently sets out a framework for leaders at all levels to build truly resilient teams, guided by values and purpose. You'll want to read it with a highlighter. I did!"

—Lori Reynolds, Lieutenant General, USMC (retired), Board Director, US Bancorp, Former Deputy Commandant for Information, USMC, and Commander, Marine Forces Cyberspace Command

"We often treat resilience as a response to crisis. This book redefines it as a proactive, cultural foundation—one that drives creativity, adaptability, and success across every metric. This book offers a clear, actionable roadmap to build resilience before you need it."

— Kim Sinatra, Strategic Advisor and Former EVP and General Counsel, Wynn Resorts. Host of "Scaling the Glass Cliff" on PRX Radio

"This book flips the script on resilience—not as a survival tactic but as a strength you intentionally build, like training a muscle. Grounded in core values, this kind of resilience doesn't just help you bounce back; it helps you lead through pressure, prevent burnout, and thrive in complexity. A must-read for leaders navigating transformative times."

— **Tracy Nolan, SVP, Humana MarketPoint**

"A must-read for any leader navigating today's high-pressure world. This book shows you how to intentionally cultivate resilience—not as a reactive tool but as a strategic, sustainable strength. Grounded, human, and immediately actionable, it's packed with sharp insights, compelling executive stories, and practical tools. I couldn't put it down—and it's already changing how I lead."

— **Sandy Fershee, Fortune 10 Design and Innovation Executive**

"Resilience is an essential skill for any leader, especially to meet the challenges of our volatile world. This book presents a novel framework for 'Intentional Resilience' that puts that skill easily within your grasp, and inspiring stories from global leaders."

— **Eve Maler, President and Founder, Venn Factory; Former CTO, ForgeRock; Co-Inventor, XML, SAML, and UMA**

"Forget bouncing back—this book is about moving forward. *Rethinking Resilience* turns uncertainty into a leadership edge. If you're leading in high-stakes, high-change environments, this is your new manual."

— **Nadia Hansen, Global Go-to-Market Executive, Keynote Speaker, Former Government CIO**

"*Rethinking Resilience* masterfully reimagines resilience for our present challenges and positions leaders for the future. It provides guidance through moments of triumph and adversity alike. Every leader navigating disruption needs to read this, now. The book is a timeless resource."

— **Ravi Shankavaram, Former CIO/CTO, New Balance Athletic Shoe, Inc.**

"*Rethinking Resilience* is a go-to guide for leaders at any point in their journey. It brings together the key leadership superpowers needed to show up with authenticity, navigate a complex world, and lead with impact. Tissa's actionable framework pulls from years of real experience, research, and coaching—and it shows. It's practical, insightful, and a resource I'll be coming back to often."

— **Wanda Hill, Vice President, Research and Development, Strategic Business Initiatives, GSK**

"This is an entirely new way to think about resilience—and why it matters in work and life. Intentional resilience isn't about toughing it out. It's about staying rooted in what matters, especially when things get messy. Since the earliest days of starting Happy Ltd, we've seen that people thrive when they feel safe, supported, and trusted—and that's where real resilience starts. *Rethinking Resilience* is a blueprint for building an Intentionally Resilient culture for your team in our disruptive world."

— **Henry Stewart, Founder and Chief Happiness Officer, Happy Ltd**

RETHINKING

FUELING
YOUR
COMPETITIVE
ADVANTAGE

RESILIENCE

TISSA RICHARDS

For Lorraine Hendrickson—
the embodiment of resilience and joy

CONTENTS

Keep building resilience:
Explore bonus tools and materials
for you and your team at
www.tissarichards.com/rethinkingresiliencebonus

INTRODUCTION

You have a competitive advantage most people don't know about.

This is how I begin the keynote I give to leaders and companies throughout the country. It didn't start as a speech, and certainly not as a book. It was born of my own hardship. After the traumatic experience of shutting down my software company—a years-long venture I had poured my savings, energy, and soul into—I discovered the Intentional Resilience I had developed within. It carried me through that devastating time and, more importantly, made me stronger than ever and ready for any new challenge.

How does Intentional Resilience differ from the traditional resilience most people know about? With Intentional Resilience, nothing passively happens *to you*; instead, growth, innovation, engagement, and adaptability happen *through you*.

I wanted to investigate Intentional Resilience further, so I interviewed finance gurus, economic experts, and military strategists—top leaders in every field—who use this approach in ways that immeasurably help them and the companies they lead.

I began to share my discovery, believing that Intentional Resilience could dramatically transform leaders, teams, and entire companies. I received immediate feedback. My audiences connected with the ideas, navigating their professional lives with more confidence and intention. Many began asking if the concepts could be applied more broadly. After all, at the end of the workday, businesspeople are just … people.

This book is, at its heart, about people. Yes, it's also about key performance indicators, artificial intelligence, and hitting quarterly targets and revenue projections. Still, at its core, it is about you: someone who can benefit from a more stress-free, engaged, and innovative life.

When Intentional Resilience is built within yourself, you'll see how it expands to your team, your business unit, and your entire company. You'll begin to recognize the characteristics we often see in Intentionally Resilient companies—conviction, curiosity, and clarity, to name a few. These companies are innovative and progressive. They ask why *and* why not. They reflect on who they want to be, repeat the actions to make it happen, and replace the old tendencies that left them stagnant.

In this book, I show you how to shift resilience from a reactive trait to an intentional strength you can use whenever and wherever you need it. In addition to actionable steps, I tell stories about remarkable leaders. They should capture your complete attention, as they did mine, and they have my gratitude.

Rethinking Resilience is not only for business applications—for the small, medium, and big-stakes situations that define your success and legacy as a leader. It is also for life's regular moments: the day-to-day, tedious, exciting, thrilling, repetitive, banal, and slightly irritating straws that can build up until they threaten to break everything. These include a last-minute request from your manager, a laptop that suddenly malfunctions, a delayed flight that makes you miss an important customer meeting, running out of your kid's favorite peanut butter, and traffic that makes you late for the dentist. You get the picture. After you read this book, you'll be able to handle anything in stride.

This book is for all of life's quirks, challenges, catastrophes, *and* opportunities. It's here to help you build a better you. I promise that Intentional Resilience will do just that.

So, where were we?

You have a competitive advantage most people don't know about.

When you rethink resilience, you choose Intentional Resilience.

You choose to be adaptable, to be engaged, and to handle whatever comes your way.

You will be successful and fulfilled. You will thrive. You will win.

Thank you.

—Tissa Richards

CHAPTER 1

RETHINKING RESILIENCE

"I am failing at resilience."

That's what she said to me, quietly but clearly, moments after I stepped off the stage. The ballroom was still humming from the keynote, with people gathering their things and checking their phones. But she stood there, holding her coffee like a lifeline, her eyes wide and honest.

"Tissa, I've read the books. I've done the journaling. I'm doing all the things they say to do. But I'm still overwhelmed. Still tired. I don't think I'm doing this resilience thing right."

And I knew exactly what she meant. Not long ago, I'd said those same words to myself. *I am failing at resilience.*

Because everything I thought resilience was supposed to be—pushing through, bouncing back, staying strong—wasn't working anymore. It wasn't holding me up. It wasn't carrying me forward.

Saying "No" to Say Yes to My Values

Years before, I stood at the helm of a fast-growing cybersecurity startup. As the founder and CEO, I was proud of our partnerships and growing patent portfolio. We were doing award-winning work. The grueling, seven-days-a-week grind was paying off.

I was traveling around the world to meet prospective customers. The team I'd assembled was cohesive, brilliant, and innovative. It seemed like my Austin, Texas-based tech startup was poised for takeoff. All my hard work and commitment were finally paying off.

Until …

We were presented with a situation by our investors that I believed challenged our founding values. I can't go into details, but I made the devastating decision to wind down the company.

It was a three-year process involving bankruptcy court and floods of letters reminding me of the massive debts I owed. Telling my team, suppliers, and clients of the closure felt like rubbing salt into an open wound. Every day, another piece of my dream crumbled before my eyes. I lost every dollar I'd invested. It was an enormous toll, both physically and emotionally. During those dark days, I felt anything but resilient. I felt like an abject failure.

And still, people called me resilient.

They said, "You bounced back so quickly." They meant it as a compliment. But it didn't feel like resilience. It felt like ruin. Quiet, epic, personal ruin. The kind you don't talk about aloud or post about online.

The Traditional View of Resilience

The term "resilience" originated in materials science, where it is used to describe how a material can absorb energy, be deformed or reshaped elastically, and then release the energy and return to its original shape and function. It can literally "bounce back" to its original form factor. Cell membranes, building materials, forests, and a variety of ecosystems are called resilient when they can withstand significant stress and recover, change, and adapt.

Over time, psychologists began to use the term to describe people who were able to cope and adapt after a painful event, such as a serious illness, accident, or divorce. We began to apply the idea of resilience to business as well, referencing teams and companies that endure setbacks and challenges by bouncing back and recovering.

We describe it in phrases like:

- Stay strong.
- Keep calm and carry on.
- Power through.
- Rebound after disruption.

This traditional view of resilience assumes adversity is the *starting point*. It kicks in after something breaks. After the layoffs. After the funding pullout. After the market crash. After the personal crisis.

It's survival-mode thinking. And while survival is necessary, it's not sustainable.

Why not? Because when we frame resilience in this way, it becomes reactive. It waits for the storm. In the reactive model, your only measures of resilience are how fast you can recover, how little you complain, how well you put a positive spin on it and fake it 'til you make it, and how quickly you get back in the saddle and back on the horse.

No wonder so many of us feel like we're doing it wrong, or like we're failing at resilience.

We're told to bounce back, even if we're still broken. To rise stronger, even when we're still raw. To show grit, even when what we really need is grace.

But what if true resilience isn't only about getting back up?

The Quest for a Better Definition

My conversation with the young woman who felt like she was failing at resilience stayed with me. So did the haunting weight of my own journey: the cost of prioritizing integrity, the silence required during the long battles, and the ache of not being able to explain it all, even to the people I loved most. My guilt was overwhelming, as were the financial setbacks.

However, I found that as a "failed" tech startup founder and CEO, I now garnered more respect in the marketplace. It was as if the closure of my business gave me street credibility. Rather than branding me as a loser, my business failure propelled my career forward. I was seen as a leader with conviction, a calculated risk-taker, and an innovator. People were interested in my business and personal stories, so I became a sought-after keynote speaker, author, executive coach, and consultant.

As I reflected, I realized that I had been building a muscle of resilience. Not just in the aftermath of the wind-down, but long before. Through the founding of the company and in the minutes, hours, days, and years I'd invested in its success. I'd made company decisions based on my values and prioritized innovation and adaptability, creating an environment of progress and growth, no matter the challenge.

Though the losses felt unbearable, I had gained something profound at the end of it all. In time, I recognized that I had gained perspective, credibility, and humility. I had gained a powerful story. Most importantly, I had gained absolute clarity about what *truly* matters.

I hadn't just "bounced back." *I thrived.* Those same elements of innovation and adaptability that I had built into my company were built into *me*, and I pushed forward to my next chapter of success, consulting with a wide variety of organizations and leaders.

A Realization

My work as an executive advisor and confidential sounding board to some of the most senior C-suite executives in the world is challenging, exhilarating, and innovative. Senior leaders from a multitude of industries come to me for guidance in navigating key decisions, inflection points, and pivots. I help leaders:

- Optimize complex decisions.
- Clarify priorities.
- Align teams.
- Communicate complexity simply and effectively.

Essentially, I help leaders navigate the challenges of *big-scale* leadership without burning out.

The challenges I guide them through are endless: A business unit GM and president of a healthcare services company was brought in to turn around a stagnant business line before a successful exit. The CEO of an innovative consumer tech company was tasked with bridging the gap between the founder's vision and the challenges of getting products to market in a scalable way—and on the investors' timeline. The board of an enterprise strategy firm was making a high-stakes expansion from large public sector clients to private sector clients in entirely new industries. Large, high-potential cohorts of senior leaders honing their strategic insights and rapidly taking on bigger scopes within their companies. And countless more.

I'm brought in to help solve high-visibility, high-dollar, high-stakes, and high-stress situations across industries and functional areas. I work directly with CEOs, CFOs, COOs, CTOs, and CIOs, giving me unique insights into their executive teams, boards of directors, and reporting lines. I have intimate familiarity with their one-, three-, and five-year strategic plans, their quarterly KPIs, and the messy realities of the performance reviews and employee metrics that reveal engagement, happiness, and organizational trust.

My front-row seat—and guiding hand—gives me a unique lens to view which leaders, teams, and companies are thriving, and which aren't. I understand who is skyrocketing into more senior roles with bigger budgets, more visibility, and more trust—and who is struggling to get a solid footing. I see which teams work with alignment, pivot rapidly, and turn disruption into opportunity. And, I see which companies emerge as winners across multiple facets: market position, revenue, stock price, regulatory goodwill, consumer trust, and innovation.

I'm honored to have this opportunity to watch my instincts about Intentional Resilience prove true, on the ground, over and over.

The companies that hardwire Intentional Resilience into their cultures, mindsets, and processes—their very DNA—don't just thrive. They win.

Instead of returning to the status quo, these companies use challenges as a catalyst for growth and productive change. They pivot quickly and innovate, even when faced with business disruptions. Company leadership at these thriving organizations displays a steadiness and comfort with change that allows them to weather the unexpected without distress. That steadiness creates a culture of confidence where challenges aren't a source of dread but a source of opportunity.

Being Intentionally Resilient can spur immense organizational growth and a host of competitive advantages.

Straight from the Trenches

In the following pages, I share my front-row seat with you and provide an easy-to-apply playbook so you can benefit from the stories and insights. This book is a look under the hood at the mindsets, systems, and behaviors that define thriving, Intentionally Resilient companies.

While I can't share all the confidential details of my work, I will share what I can. I asked leaders from around the world—across industries, functional areas, countries, and continents—to share their insights and stories as well. And they did, generously. You'll hear from remarkable executives at companies as varied as the S&P Global, Nasdaq, Walmart, The Campbell's Company, Citi, Accenture, Dolce & Gabbana, Wipro, Franklin Templeton, and Sam's Club, plus commercial rocket companies, fast-growth startups, and some of the most senior members of the United States military.

In dozens of interviews, we covered topics from complex business issues, innovation amid challenges, and deeply impactful personal events. The leaders I interviewed don't just survive their challenges; they leverage them. They embed Intentional Resilience into how they lead, communicate, and make decisions.

The stories and examples will show you that these successful leaders don't wait for a moment of crisis. Instead, they systematically design their teams and organizations so they are proactively prepared *no matter what happens.*

Rather than displaying resilience only during hard days, these leaders hardwire it into their teams continuously so that when challenges arise, everyone is ready with the right mindset and the right skill set. The most successful leaders don't wait to bounce *back*: they intentionally build in the capacity to move *forward*.

And you can, too.

Resilience Isn't Soft

One of the most damaging misconceptions about resilience is that it's a "soft" skill. Emotional. Intangible. Optional. But that could not be further from the truth.

Resilience directly impacts speed to decision, risk tolerance, employee retention, innovation cycles, and strategic focus. It shows up in investor confidence, board trust, and team morale.

It's the difference between a leadership team that freezes and one that adapts, an organization that spins in confusion and one that recalibrates rapidly.

Intentionally Resilient leaders and companies share commonalities:

- They don't over-identify with one solution, one org chart, or one way of working.
- They build flexibility into their systems.
- They normalize iteration.
- They listen early, not just in a postmortem.
- They use tension as a design input.

I've watched clients go through massive challenges and emerge stronger than before because they were willing to pivot 5 to 10 percent every week. They repurposed, reassigned, and reclarified *while they were in motion.*

When I coach senior leaders, I observe how well their teams execute under pressure. But I also watch for a more critical indicator: how quickly those teams recover from friction. Performance is no longer only about the output. It's about the velocity of your recovery.

The best teams I've seen inside startups, global conglomerates, non-profits, and Fortune 500 boardrooms use Intentional Resilience to do three things differently:

1. **They metabolize change fast.** They don't wait to be told how to adapt. They look for the adjustment early. They recalibrate plans mid-cycle and treat tension as data, not as dysfunction.

2. **They communicate clearly and often.** Not just downward, but laterally and upward, as well. They normalize check-ins, ask better questions, and signal shifts early.

3. **They regulate emotion without suppressing it.** They don't shame stress; they build psychological safety around it. And when the heat rises, they stay responsive, not reactive.

That's not luck. That's intentional.

Wanted: A Competitive Advantage

We're not living in steady-state times.

Markets are volatile—close to home and globally. Workplaces are evolving. AI is changing the landscape. Leaders are under pressure to grow, adapt, and innovate all at once (and often in public). In a world where complexity is the norm, resilience can no longer be seen as an emergency response. It must be part of the operating model, intentionally baked into everyday operations.

The business world is more demanding than ever. In the last few years, we've been shaken up by so many "unprecedented events" that instability is now the norm. Between supply chain disruptions, tariffs, accelerating natural disasters, and a volatile stock market, it's more challenging to create a high-functioning team, meet KPIs, and stand out in a competitive marketplace.

- What if it were possible to expand your personal strengths and leadership skills so you could stop feeling overwhelmed and burned out? *It is.*
- What if you could foster a culture where teams communicate effectively, reach alignment, and find innovative solutions? *You can.*

- What if you could take small steps today that would insulate your organization from the damage caused by outside events and hard-wire an ability to pivot, adapt, and profit—faster and easier? *You can.*

In the following chapters, I'll share the mindsets, behaviors, and play-books of Intentionally Resilient leaders who are more than traditionally resilient. These C-suite executives, founders, and innovators have an edge that sets them apart. They've discovered how to take smarter risks, adapt faster, uncover opportunities, and retain talent longer.

Imagine what you could do with that knowledge. Imagine the competitive advantage you could deploy for yourself, your team, and your company.

Resilience Across Ecosystems

We all operate simultaneously in distinct ecosystems—our homes, our workplaces, and our communities. Each ecosystem demands slightly different skills and approaches. For example, you communicate differently with your partner than with your direct reports. The negotiation skills you use at the office may come in handy in your neighborhood home-owners' association, but you must apply them differently.

It's clear that the most successful leaders—those who embrace the approach of Intentional Resilience—perform better, experience less conflict, and make a deeper impact in *all* their ecosystems. They still deal with demanding situations, but they do so with less drama and less stress.

In my work with Intentionally Resilient leaders, I notice that while their lives are no less challenging than others' lives, they navigate those challenges with less friction across every ecosystem. They demonstrate a unique form of resilience that exceeds our current understanding of the term. Intentional Resilience gives them a competitive advantage, which they apply to their personal and professional lives.

Read On to Win

By the time you finish this book, you will have gained a playbook for this new model of resilience, which breaks down silos, creates opportunities, and produces extraordinary results. We'll explore the seven core components that contribute to Intentional Resilience. Each one is a lever for growth and competitive advantage.

And here's great news: You *already* have Intentional Resilience. If you've been living, leading, and working, and if you've been handling the beautiful challenges, opportunities, and complexities of life, you've got this. (You just might not be aware of it yet.)

I'm not offering you abstract ideals or impossible tasks that will add to your stress. Instead, you'll gain a proactive mindset—and the accompanying skills—that will strengthen over time, becoming a catalyst for growth and innovation. You'll discover simple tools you can use—and take back to your team—for challenging times and the everyday moments that matter. These tools will help you make an impact as a leader who can innovate through any challenge.

Intentional Resilience isn't something you *wait for*. You deliberately *design for it*.

Let's begin.

CHAPTER 2

SWIPE RIGHT FOR INTENTIONAL RESILIENCE

Ice packs have been particularly important in my life. I have a rare health condition where I don't produce all the digestive enzymes my body needs; it's an "orphan disease" that affects fewer than two hundred thousand people in the US. For over fifteen years, I've received a refrigerated medication shipment every three weeks that includes several ice packs. I hate throwing out so many ice packs, but I can only keep so many extras in my freezer.

About a year ago, I noticed the ice packs had new printing on them. "Plant food … dilute with water and feed to your plants!" I was intrigued because innovation doesn't usually work that way.

Let's examine innovation for a minute. Except for enormous companies that have budgets for innovation labs, innovation is usually a response to negative external pressure:

- "Our biggest competitor is about to do X, so we should do it also."
- "Regulators will require us to take action soon, so it would be smart to change our product or business model to get ahead."
- "Economic pressures are impacting our margins, so we need to adapt our product or service to cut costs."

It's rare for a company to innovate without that negative external pressure. But that ice pack I received was rare. So, I reached out to the company, Pelton Shepherd Industries, and its CEO, Tim Shepherd.

Tim doesn't talk about innovation as a buzzword. He treats it as a responsibility.

In the 1950s, Tim's grandfather Jack Shepherd invented a way to keep ice frozen on local ice cream delivery routes. Over the decades, Jack's company, Pelton Shepherd Industries, expanded into creating hard packs nestled into the tops of coolers, gel packs for physical therapy, and a variety of other methods for shipping perishables safely. Tim's father served as the CEO, and Tim started working on the company's shop floor in his teens. The small company maintained a trusted position in a very niche industry until the advent of the internet and online shopping. Suddenly, the world had a growing demand for temperature-sensitive gel packs to ship medications, food, and other perishables.

By then, Tim was the third generation to lead Pelton Shepherd Industries, overseeing a tremendous surge in demand as more consumers became accustomed to online shopping. He started to wonder what people were doing with all those gel packs, and he found that most of them were thrown away and ended up in landfills.

The Pelton Shepherd values are clear: Always do the right thing for customers and the planet. In this case, Tim and his team, including Sylvain Marseille, VP of Marketing and New Product Development, began exploring alternative options that would be more environmentally friendly. Eventually, they developed ice packs made from material that can be used as a plant food. Now, instead of filling up garbage cans and landfills with discarded ice packs, consumers can reuse the material from the packs in their houseplants and gardens. The company has also developed a variety of fully compostable ice packs that will degrade faster, making it the greenest ice pack manufacturer in the country.

"We weren't required to focus on safe sustainability by law or regulation," Tim shared. "We just decided it was the right thing to do for our customers and the planet. Our company is based on trust, so we want our ice packs to demonstrate that we care and act in a trustworthy way." No urgent market pressure pushed the company to add these ice packs to the product catalog. Tim and his team replaced the traditional *reactive* innovation with *intentional* innovation: ice packs that become plant food and are drain-safe and fully biodegradable.

The company continues to innovate, seeking a replacement for dry ice and other ways to cool products for shipping with a lower environmental impact. Tim said, "When you set your compass to doing the right thing for your customer, you always end up winning."

Pelton Shepherd is an outstanding example of an Intentionally Resilient company. It's nimble, able to absorb market fluctuations, and focuses on constant innovation while still delivering profits to shareholders. Tim has created a culture where employees at every level are encouraged to share ideas for improvements in processes, marketing, and product development.

He believes the company has an edge over its competitors because of its long history and stable leadership, which includes his sister Ali Shepherd Reising, who serves as the Senior VP of Customer Relations and Logistics. The company's tagline highlights its value: "Trusted when temperature matters." By inspiring the team to think differently and find solutions to challenges *before* those challenges become problems, Pelton Shepherd not only embraces change but also nurtures and depends on it.

This is a competitive advantage beyond a product perspective. In years to come, regulators or the market may demand environmentally friendly products, and Pelton Shepherd is already there. Employees know the company is living its stated values, and customers—like me—are delighted. Intentional Resilience, in this case, has created intentional innovation, along with a whole host of other competitive advantages.

Pelton Shepherd has all the earmarks that come naturally to companies with Intentional Resilience: clear values, proactive innovation, and an ability to transform everyday challenges into opportunities. While others are paralyzed, waiting for certainty, Intentionally Resilient organizations like Pelton Shepherd are experimenting, adapting, and capturing opportunities their competitors can't even see.

The Pelton Shepherd story is a perfect example of Intentional Resilience in action.

What Biology Teaches Us About Resilience

In biology, resilience isn't about toughness. It's about permeability.

Take a cell membrane. Its job isn't to be a wall. It's to regulate what comes in, what stays out, and how the internal system adapts. A resilient membrane doesn't shut everything out. It allows nutrients in, expels waste, and adapts to stress.

Too rigid? The cell can't take in what it needs. Too porous? It gets overwhelmed. In the same way that cell membranes filter nutrients while keeping harmful agents out, resilient people and organizations learn to let in only what strengthens them, especially during times of stress or crisis when our instinct is often to shut down, harden, and block things out. But the most Intentionally Resilient people I know do something else. They stay permeable. They let in support. They receive perspective. They metabolize hard moments instead of storing them.

They just don't *survive* the pressure; they grow stronger *because* of it.

Intentional Resilience is not about bracing for impact. It's about staying open to what helps you evolve—even in the middle of the storm.

The Collapse That Clarified Everything

When I shut down my company, I thought I was making the bravest move possible by standing in integrity, choosing my values over investor pressure, and walking away from a business I loved.

In many ways, it was brave. But no one had warned me about what came next.

I had court dates. IRS letters. Friends who turned into strangers overnight. I had to sell my house to make ends meet. My parents divorced, and my father stopped speaking to me because of the stress over our enormous debts. I couldn't explain what happened, legally or emotionally. Yet, the world kept turning as if nothing had shifted, while everything in me had.

I kept waiting for the "resilient" part to kick in. That triumphant, bounce-back moment. But it never showed up, at least not in the way I expected.

Instead, what showed up was a slower, quieter, and much more powerful experience: a new understanding that I could be resilient even though I would not bounce back to "business as usual." Instead, I could grow through the challenge, reimagine a different career, and seize the new opportunities amid the chaos.

The Two Types of Resilience

Most people think of resilience the way they think of seat belts, which only become useful in a crash. We've been taught that resilience is what kicks in *after* the hardship: the comeback story, the badge of honor, and the tear-streaked-but-determined moment of perseverance.

Let's call this the first type of resilience: *Reactive Resilience*. It's necessary, it has its place, but it's limited. Reactive Resilience is about returning to the baseline and coping, holding it all together, and holding *yourself* together.

Simply put, you're faced with a challenge, and you have to work to restore the situation to its original state. It's the ability to recover after a product failure, disaster, loss of a primary client, or even an unexpected surge in the popularity of your offerings. (It's not always a reaction to a negative stimulus, but it's always a *reaction*!)

Consider your body's nerves. When they receive a stimulus, they fire automatically. You burn your finger on a hot stove, and your hand moves reflexively away from the pain. A challenge arrives, and you find a solution.

In a business setting, Reactive Resilience sounds like:

- "I can't wait for this situation to get back to normal."
- "As soon as this crisis is over, I'm going to deal with X (insert that nagging problem or person you don't have time to address right now)."

- "We've got a situation here. I'm going to need all hands on deck."
- "Where's our disaster manual?"

But you can develop another type of resilience—one that doesn't wait for the breakdown to begin.

Another Option: Intentional Resilience

Reactive Resilience is like a nerve—it fires automatically when the stimulus hits. It's instinctive. It's survival mode. And while it's useful in a crisis, its value is limited. It only activates *after* something goes wrong.

Intentional Resilience is different. You train it like a muscle *before* the challenge arrives—through habits, culture, and design. And when the pressure comes, you don't just endure the stress—you move through it with focus and direction.

As I worked with extraordinary leaders across industries and countries, one pattern stood out: They didn't wait for problems to arise. They prepared for them. They created systems that could adapt, teams that could flex, and cultures that could see possibilities even amid uncertainty. They weren't just reacting, they were building Intentional Resilience into the bones of the business.

You can feel it in the communication of their teams. In the questions they ask in interviews. In the way decisions are made, meetings are run, and ideas are tested. It shows up in the systems they build and the signals they send—every day, not only in emergencies.

Intentional Resilience isn't about bouncing *back*. It's about moving *forward*. It turns challenge into clarity, adversity into advantage, and pressure into power and performance.

And here's the good news: Intentional Resilience is a mindset. Think of it like a skill and a set of practices you can learn, strengthen, and scale for yourself, your team, and your organization.

You will not only survive the storm but also learn to lead through it and grow because of it.

The Other Side of Resilience

Reactive Resilience	Intentional Resilience
Waits for disruption	Anticipates friction
Reacts under pressure	Plans under pressure
Responds emotionally	Regulates early and often
Prioritizes recovery	Prioritizes clarity and alignment
Hopes to bounce back	Designed to foster growth

Life Doesn't Happen to You; Growth Happens Through You

We've all seen it before: When a crisis or disruption hits, many people go into reactive mode. Leaders, teams, and companies that operate in the traditional Reactive Resilience model are where you'll hear phrases like:

- "We don't know why this is happening to us."
- "How are we supposed to handle this?"
- "What will this mean?"

This model is about passivity and reactivity and a sense that challenges—external forces and factors—are happening *to you*, forcing you to go into crisis response mode. It's all too common, and when I workshop the shift from Reactive Resilience to Intentional Resilience with teams, I help them see that every challenge carries within it the seeds of innovation, clarity, and growth. But only if you're equipped to recognize and use them. That's what Intentional Resilience unlocks.

It's the shift from feeling like life is happening *to* you, to realizing that growth can happen *through* you. The shift ignites interesting questions and curiosity:

- "What is possible?"
- "How can we respond to this rapidly and positively?"
- "What opportunities could this spark?"

I've seen it in leaders who've faced layoffs, political upheaval, failed launches, personal challenges, and everything in between. The ones who grow aren't the ones who avoid hardship; they're the ones who are equipped to move with it with curiosity and openness.

They have a toolkit. A language. A rhythm. They don't just bounce back, they move forward. Their growth is relational because even the strongest personal resilience needs reinforcement. Leaders don't thrive in isolation. They move forward faster—and with more clarity—when Intentional Resilience is distributed across a team as a *shared* strength, not just the leader's strength.

Intentional Resilience Is Shared

One of the most persistent myths in business is the idea of the lone resilient hero: the leader who shoulders it all, never flinches, powers through, and always bounces back. It makes for a great social media post. But in reality? That's not how resilience works.

Intentional Resilience is a shared practice. Research backs this up. Supportive environments change our biochemistry as oxytocin rises and cortisol drops, reducing the activation of our amygdala—our brain's fear detector. There's power and peace in being supported by others. We regulate each other—even in silence.

I saw this in my own company. One day, our engineering team proposed a major product pivot. It would delay a customer delivery by months, but it would better serve future clients in the pipeline. The "old me"—who was exhausted and in survival mode—might have shut it down fast. But because we had trust, because we had a shared language and values, I listened.

We made the pivot, and it worked.

This was Intentional Resilience in action—distributed, relational, and real. Whether it's a teammate's Slack message, a walk with a mentor, or your toddler's hand in yours when the world feels overwhelming, these moments are part of the fabric of shared resilience. And for leaders, building that fabric is part of the job.

The 3 R's of Intentional Resilience

Shared resilience is powerful, and it works best when each person brings a grounded foundation. For me, that foundation came into focus during one of the most challenging chapters of my life. It's where I discovered the habits that held me steady.

I call them the 3 R's: Reflect. Repeat. Replace.

Reflect

I didn't shut down my company in one dramatic moment. That decision came after months of quiet reflection—about the business I was building, the kind of CEO I wanted to be, and the values I wasn't willing to compromise.

Reflection isn't passive. It's a discipline. It means pausing long enough to see clearly and choose wisely. I had already made those choices long before—about who I hired, which companies we partnered with, and how I handled conflict. Like the time a potential partner berated both our teams during a call. I paused the meeting and said, "Let's regroup when everyone's calm, because one of our core values is respect, and that value is not being honored right now."

That wasn't reactive. It was rooted. That was Intentional Resilience, in real time.

Repeat

Intentional Resilience becomes powerful when repeated. I hadn't named it yet, but I'd been practicing it all along. Small daily choices—how I communicated, how I led, and how I reinforced culture—created a rhythm. That rhythm became Intentional Resilience. It wasn't a heroic response but a habit built through consistent, values-aligned action. Repetition is how you build muscle memory that becomes second nature.

Replace

When everything felt like it was falling apart, I had to reframe what was happening to move forward. To shift from Reactive Resilience to

Intentional Resilience. I had to replace fear with purpose, loss with learning, and control with clarity.

I had to see it as growth happening *through* me, not an event happening *to* me. That mindset didn't erase my grief, but it helped me lead forward with integrity and gain insights I wouldn't have found in success alone.

The Power of Small Wins

Those three habits helped me stay grounded. However, Intentional Resilience isn't always about navigating a crisis. Sometimes, it's about navigating the long, slow road and keeping your sense of progress along the way.

Charles Newnam knows something about that. Today, Charles is a Principal Director at Accenture, where he leads talent, leadership, and culture transformations. Before entering the world of consulting, Charles served as a US Navy submarine officer, operating in high-stakes environments that demanded calm under pressure, exceptional teamwork, and relentless endurance.

As a submarine officer, he spent months below the ocean's surface with no sunlight, no fresh air, and no visible markers of time. The hardest part wasn't the emergencies, it was the sameness, the routine, and the quiet drain of not knowing whether the effort was getting anywhere.

So, Charles began a small ritual: Each night, he and his crew moved a tiny plastic submarine one hinge forward on a metal panel in the sub's control room, marking one more day complete. One hinge closer to the mission's success. One hinge closer to home.

"It was just a piece of plastic," he told me. "But it reminded us that we were moving. That today counted."

It didn't change the mission, but it changed the mindset. It gave the crew visible proof of progress, even when the journey felt long. Charles still uses the practice of measuring small wins and progress. On trails where he runs ultramarathons, in boardrooms, and anywhere momentum can be made visible.

Intentional Resilience isn't about grit, it's about pace and proof and giving yourself daily evidence that effort matters, even in small ways.

Micro-Moments: Where the Real Work Happens

We tend to over-glorify big wins and dramatic turnarounds, but the real building blocks of Intentional Resilience are incredibly ordinary. Perhaps you have:

- Rewritten a heated email after walking around the block.
- Chosen to listen instead of reacting in a tough meeting.
- Set a boundary with kindness, even when it was uncomfortable.

If so, then you've already practiced Intentional Resilience. It's forged in the moments you almost overlook. These are what I call **micro-moments**: small, intentional actions that move you forward mentally, emotionally, or physically, even when the big goal feels out of reach. (Just like Charles moving a tiny plastic submarine.)

Micro-moments aren't breakthroughs, they're nudges. They're quiet signals that say: "I'm still in motion. I haven't stopped." When practiced consistently, they build trust with others and with yourself.

Leaders who embed Intentional Resilience into their cultures don't wait for crises. They design micro-moments into the rhythm of the work, such as:

- A weekly "win roundup" to celebrate momentum.
- A quick "What's one thing I can help you with this week?" check-in.
- A standing meeting that ends with, "What failure can we learn from today?"

These are hinges, not grand gestures. And over time, they move the entire system forward.

Micro-moments become the muscle memory for how we lead under pressure. They shape how your team sees you, and how they show up when it counts.

One leader I interviewed built an unshakable foundation of Intentional Resilience through a lifetime of micro-moments. In the next section, you'll see how every one of those moments—personal and professional—added up.

A Lifetime of Personal Intentional Resilience

Elissar Farah Antonios has built her life and leadership in regions where uncertainty is the norm, not the exception. A Lebanese-UAE national, she's lived through war zones, political instability, and economic shocks—while also rising through the ranks to become a banking CEO, global board member, investor, and mentor to the next generation of leaders.

After pivoting from her role as CEO of Citi UAE, Elissar now leads a portfolio career with three clear pillars: active investment through her firm Soul Ventures Holding, board service in public and nonprofit organizations, and global advocacy for leadership development—especially for women navigating complex, high-pressure careers. In all three roles, she demonstrates Intentional Resilience as her compass because she's had to be resilient her entire life.

Elissar grew up in Lebanon, where war was part of daily life. Resilience was how you lived. She told me, "If something catastrophic happens today, you pick up the pieces and move forward. And if something else happens tomorrow, you do it again. And again. And again."

During Elissar's tenure at Citi, she was attending a meeting in London when a massive and unanticipated power outage caused panic among her UK-based senior leader peers. They had no idea how to function without electricity because an outage of that magnitude had never happened before. Elissar was calm—this situation was nothing new to her. She'd grown up with near-constant power outages. She calmed her peers down, pragmatically suggested they bring in power generators, and brought rapid, practical solutions and stability.

Elissar believes that although Intentional Resilience isn't taught in school, it can be developed over time in four steps:

1. Clearly define your goals and the strategy to achieve them.

2. Be agile and ready to adapt to changing conditions. Companies that are agile outperform their competition.

3. Create deep bonds of trust within your teams to eliminate second-guessing. Strengthen trust by standing with your team in both good times and difficult ones.

4. Put any items that you can't control "in a box" so you can focus on areas where you can make an impact.

Elissar's career has taken her into some of the most volatile markets in the world, regions where her team had to navigate bombings, civil unrest, and economic instability. Through it all, she's led with a focused, steady calm. That steadiness is intentional. It's the product of resilience built deliberately through discipline, reflection, and design.

As you've seen, leaders like Elissar and Tim from Pelton Shepherd don't just survive pressure; they shape it. They build teams that are grounded, agile, and ready because their resilience isn't reactive. It's a strategic edge, not a soft skill.

Whether you're competing for a corner office, venture capital funding, or market share, your ability to respond under pressure—without losing your center—is your advantage. That's what Intentional Resilience gives you: the clarity to move forward, even in uncertainty. The composure to make decisions when others panic. The presence to lead when it counts most.

Once you begin to build it, that resilience reinforces itself powerfully and becomes a flywheel—one that accelerates growth, energy, and impact.

In the next chapter, I'll show you how the flywheel came to life through my work guiding leaders and teams, grounded in real leadership behavior. What began as repeated insights became a system. And that system allows leaders not just to withstand pressure, but to lead through it—by design.

CHAPTER 3

THE FLYWHEEL

"How can we use your model of Intentional Resilience to select the best CEO for the company?"

A year ago, a longtime client of mine, Jim, retired from the executive leadership team of a large public company and became a board director for two companies. I helped him navigate his exit, his board journey, and his onboarding to board service. Jim then asked me to help one of his boards optimize the CEO hiring process to select for Intentional Resilience.

I'm asked a variation of this question frequently. Once people realize the competitive advantages that flow from Intentional Resilience, they want to hire for it, wire it into their cultures, and build it into their organizational DNA.

As you learned in Chapter 1, I have the privilege of working with many Intentionally Resilient teams and organizations. I have a front-row seat to what works—and what doesn't.

When I answer questions like Jim's—in fireside chats after keynotes, in workshops, and in consulting engagements—I think about the qualities that Intentionally Resilient leaders possess.

At the beginning of any engagement, I ask a series of questions to senior leadership. They include:

- What is the strength of your point of view on strategy and desired outcomes?
- How strong is your conviction of this point of view when you are challenged by stakeholders or the board?
- What are your leadership values? Why?
- How do those values lead directly to desired outcomes?
- How do you communicate with stakeholders in a variety of situations that require clarity and flexibility?

I ask for concrete examples. The answers reveal a lot about the leader or the leadership team.

Patterns emerge—decisiveness, adaptability, emotional composure, clarity in crisis, and team-level trust.

I can identify which leaders and leadership teams will adapt effectively under pressure, lead through uncertainty, and still create momentum. They have conviction and focus, and they operate with a rhythm, cadence, and clarity of motion. They aim for repeatability, not rigidity, and they communicate precisely and flexibly.

These descriptions kept cropping up as I guided Jim in his board's CEO search and in my conversations with others. After a few years of seeing this pattern, I knew a framework was coalescing: a more formal description of the leaders, teams, and companies that I would categorize as Intentionally Resilient.

So, I distilled the pattern into a model with seven core components. All deeply human. All learnable. And all interconnected.

Intentional Resilience, I realized, isn't linear; it doesn't follow a step-by-step checklist. It builds, compounds, and creates energy when each piece is aligned.

When I stepped back to examine it more closely, I realized it wasn't a list or framework after all. It was a flywheel—a living force with energy at its center. A mechanism that, once set in motion, sustains itself power-fully. And that's where the model came to life.

That's what Intentional Resilience is about. It's not a reaction, but a rhythm. It's a system you build into how you lead, how you make decisions, and how you recover. And once you feel it working, you don't want to lead any other way.

The Seven Components of the Flywheel

Intentional Resilience isn't powered by one trait or tool. It's built through a set of interconnected components that reinforce each other over time. Through years of coaching, research, and leadership development, I kept seeing the same seven elements appear in the most Intentionally Resilient, innovative leaders and in the cultures they shaped.

These seven dimensions form the flywheel: a self-sustaining system that builds power through consistency and alignment. Each one plays a distinct role—how we lead ourselves, how we lead others, and how our leadership fuels the success of an entire company. Together, they form a dynamic system in which progress in one area strengthens the others.

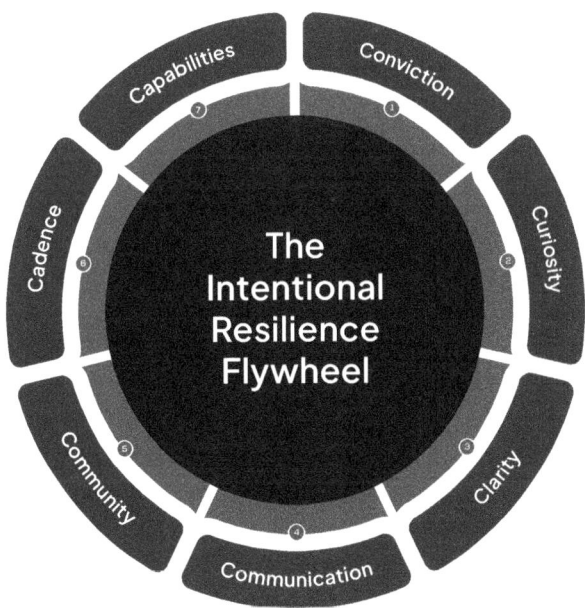

Here's a brief look at each component and how it functions collaboratively to create Intentional Resilience by design.

1. **Conviction:** The mindset that anchors you during uncertainty. It's the ability to keep moving when there's no applause and no map, holding to your values in high-stakes situations and standing firm. That's what conviction looks like—aligned tenacity.

2. **Curiosity:** The habit of asking better questions. It sounds simple, but in practice, it's radical. Curiosity keeps you from defaulting to old playbooks. It gives your team permission to learn, evolve, and challenge assumptions—even in the face of uncertainty—without fear of punishment. It's a posture of constant openness that keeps you learning.

3. **Clarity:** The ability to filter noise and act on what matters most. In the heat of a launch, a crisis, or a team conflict, clarity is the skill that allows leaders to say, "This is what we're doing, and why." It's the opposite of chaos—finding a clear signal and priority despite the noise and pressure.

4. **Communication:** The transmission of trust. This isn't about being the loudest voice in the room but about making others feel seen and safe enough to share what's real, especially when what's real is messy.

5. **Community:** The relationships that hold us. When Intentional Resilience is a shared practice, teams can carry more together than any one person can alone. This looks like mutual accountability, deep listening, and a bias toward connection in moments of stress.

6. **Cadence:** The rhythm of action and recovery. Intentionally Resilient cultures understand tempo. They know when to sprint, when to jog, and when to pause and recalibrate. It's not a hustle, it's an intentional, optimized tempo.

7. **Capabilities:** The mindsets, tools, and skills that turn values into action. This is where the playbook meets the real world: it's the tools you need to model and reinforce Intentional Resilience daily for your team and for yourself.

Each component feeds the others. When one gets stronger, the others often follow. That's what makes it a flywheel instead of a checklist. In a world of disruption and fatigue, the flywheel offers a rare value: a framework leaders can build into their organizations—one that increases in power and impact with use.

Why Not Momentum?

I wrestled with the word "momentum." It's popular in leadership circles, but it doesn't fit here. Momentum often implies speed for speed's sake. Once it starts, it keeps rolling—downhill, if necessary.

But the Intentional Resilience flywheel doesn't roll without aim. It doesn't just spin faster. It spins *stronger*.

That's why the flywheel is the clearest model of Intentional Resilience. The energy built here is stored for strategic release. It's about capacity, not urgency. You build the reserve so that when the pressure hits, you activate instead of collapsing. You create instead of just responding.

The Flywheel in Action

Derek Penn grew up in Youngstown, Ohio. He had no silver spoons and no shortcuts in life, just his focus, values, and the kind of determination that starts early and never lets go. He worked hard and won a football scholarship to Duke University.

It was challenging to play Division I football while keeping up with his classes. When his grade point average (GPA) dropped to 1.9 in his sophomore year at Duke, he didn't spiral. He planned. "I told myself, 'I'm not going to let this be my story. I am not going home a failure.'"

He mapped out every class he'd need to graduate, and worked his way back to a better GPA, eventually graduating with a double major in chemistry and English while playing Division I football—an impressive feat.

After a short stint in the National Football League, Derek earned his MBA and launched a thirty-four-year career on Wall Street, starting at a time when few African Americans worked on the trading floor. In time, he rose to the executive level, managing equity trading teams through market chaos.

The environment was always volatile, as markets rise and fall based on uncontrollable factors. Derek focused on what could be controlled. He became known for his calm nature. He made sure his teams knew what mattered, what didn't, and where to act.

"Panic is contagious," he said. "So is calm."

When one of his highest-performing traders started melting down emotionally, Derek didn't look away. He sat him down and said, "We're not going to win like that. You're too good to lead like this."

Today, he serves on the board of the Charles Schwab Mutual Fund and exchange-traded products complex, several nonprofit boards, and a startup that navigates the tension between ambition and uncertainty. He's also the author of *Diary of a Black Man on Wall Street*, a book he thought would sell a hundred copies but that became a bestseller that opened many new conversations.

Across all his professional endeavors, Derek reinforces a powerful truth: Intentional Resilience is individual, but it is not solitary. You build it with people, and then you reinforce it through action.

Kim Nakamaru thrives in places where most people panic. As the General Counsel of Relativity Space—a rocket startup redefining the future of aerospace—she leads the legal, environmental health and safety, corporate security, and employee relations functions. A lifelong athlete, Kim believes leadership skills are built by time and repetition, then strengthened by navigating life and work with mental toughness, purpose, and flow.

Kim lives inside complexity. The volume of decisions she faces daily would flatten a less-experienced leader. But she doesn't rush. Instead, she orients. "I don't have time to second-guess every move. I have to start from my North Star," she said. Kim's North Star is her values, which help her quickly make decisions.

Kim learned from a colleague the power of quiet confidence in high-stakes moments: "Sometimes you just have to 'sit your chair.' Don't rush to fill the silence. Gather yourself. Then respond." Her style isn't loud, but when she speaks, people listen.

When a bet-the-company reorganization landed mid-rocket-build, Kim didn't panic. She paused, realigned, and then communicated with transparency. "I told my team what I knew, what I didn't, and what we'd figure out together."

As a current triathlete and former swimmer, soccer player, and college rower, Kim knows when to push, when and how to find flow, and when to stop for a breath. That rhythm isn't just a wellness practice; it's a leadership skill.

Her resilience is about system intelligence and coolness under pressure, made repeatable.

Intentional Resilience by Design: Culture, Not Just Character

Resilience is often framed as a personal trait. However, in every high-functioning system I've studied—from elite trading desks to cross-border teams—the real power emerges when Intentional Resilience extends beyond the individual. That's when it becomes a design.

An Intentionally Resilient culture doesn't rely on heroes but instead distributes capacity and strengthens through shared language, rituals, and expectations. The flywheel is a method, not just a model, and you can feel it when it's working.

Let's look deeper. If Derek represents grounded clarity, Kim offers flow-state focus, global complexity, and agility. Their personalities and domains are different. They each use all seven of the components in the flywheel differently. But the underlying throughline? Strikingly similar. That's the power of this model, which transcends personality. It spans across industries, geographies, and titles. It's not about who you *are* but about what you've *built*. And it's not about what happens *to* you but about what growth and insights you actively cultivate *through* you.

Here are concrete examples of each of the seven core components in action:

- **Conviction:** When Derek raised his GPA from 1.9 to hitting high marks in a dual degree, it wasn't about ego, it was about vision. That kind of conviction inspires entire teams.
- **Curiosity:** Kim's ability to lead through global complexity rests on her willingness to listen deeply, ask better questions, and stay open. She doesn't assume she knows and instead stays in motion, learning as she leads.
- **Clarity:** Derek's calm confrontation with his trader didn't shame— it clarified. Kim uses her North Star to filter decisions fast. That clarity multiplies under pressure.
- **Communication:** On the trading floor, Derek knew that panic spreads. He stayed calm, factual, and future-facing when communicating with his team. Kim tries to pause and gather her thoughts before she speaks to ensure her message is thoughtful and well-received.
- **Community:** Derek mentors with humility. Kim surfaces and articulates uncertainty so her team doesn't shoulder it alone. Both lead by creating safety for others.
- **Cadence:** Neither Kim nor Derek sprints every mile. They both honor the rhythm of sustainable leadership—work and rest, tension and reset.
- **Capabilities:** Both Derek and Kim built the habits, systems, and language to perform under pressure. Resilience isn't a fluke. It's practiced and built in.

Your Turn

Every leader has some version of these seven components. You would not have reached a leadership position without them. However, there's a good chance you haven't been consciously aware of them.

As our world becomes increasingly complex and unpredictable, today's leaders require a more focused approach to their personal and team development. The old ways of working, achieving, and leading are no longer sufficient for us to thrive today. Our new world demands innovation, agility, and the ability to seize opportunities much faster than ever before. **Intentional Resilience is no longer optional.**

In the chapters ahead, we'll take a closer look at each component, starting with conviction and how it drives real-world Intentional Resilience. My goal is to give you and your team a competitive advantage.

CHAPTER 4

CONVICTION—THE MINDSET OF OPPORTUNITY

Two days into a new Group Vice President role, a high-stakes decision landed on Archana Arunkumar's desk. As a technology executive who has led large-scale transformations across product and engineering organizations, Archana is no stranger to high-stakes decisions. She has worked at companies including UKG, Expedia Group, Workday, Dropbox, Ellie Mae, and Dell EMC, and is a board director at Kwik Lok, a privately held company that manufactures packaging solutions used globally for many consumer and industrial products.

In the case of this high-stakes decision, she said, "I had just come in. I hadn't even met half my leadership team in person yet."

It was a strategic shift in a critical market. The numbers were aggressive. The internal debate had been swirling for weeks before she arrived. And now it was on her to make the call, with no grace period. No warm-up lap.

She made the decision. She weighed the data, took a breath, and trusted what she knew in her gut. Then she brought the team into alignment, not with bravado, but with confidence in her decision. "I told them, 'Here's what we're doing, and here's why. And if it turns out we need to pivot, we will. But we're not going to stall.'"

A few weeks later, one of her senior directors came to her. The director, who was managing more than two hundred people globally, felt overwhelmed and was drowning. Archana had a choice. She could take the conventional route: lighten his workload, reassign projects, and help him stabilize. But Archana trusted the data and trusted what the data wasn't yet showing.

Instead of removing responsibilities, she did something counterintuitive. She added *more* to his plate. Archana gave him a new initiative. It was a project with a different team, with a distinct set of dynamics and a fresh set of problems to solve. From the outside, it looked risky. From the inside, Archana had already been tracking signs of stalled innovation and creeping burnout. She knew that cognitive fatigue often doesn't stem from too *much* work but from too much of the same *kind* of work. So, she bet on variety.

Two weeks later, her gamble paid off. The director came back energized, clearer, and surprisingly more productive. "I don't know what I was thinking," he admitted to Archana. "I thought I was drowning, but I actually have more bandwidth now."

Archana hadn't been guessing. She had looked at the key metrics: code push rates, bug reports, postmortem participation, and velocity. Data told her what emotion couldn't: when resistance was rising, when innovation was stalling, and when her teams were operating from fear rather than curiosity.

In Archana's world, conviction doesn't come from a gut feeling alone. It comes from patterns. From noticing when the same old solutions no longer yield results. From spotting when psychological safety is eroding, not just through feedback sessions but through slowdowns in code delivery or upticks in errors or rework.

"It's trust, but verify," she said. "I trust my teams. But I also track real-time data: customer feedback, churn rate, productivity signals. That way, I don't have to dive into the weeds to know what's going on. The system tells me."

This philosophy helped her lead transformations in the AI space and implement company-wide shifts without triggering cultural backlash. Whether creating a "tech council" of senior engineers to crowdsource priorities or prompting teams to write up and share learnings internally, Archana uses data not just to justify change but to invite people into it.

Data, for her, isn't about control but about clarity. It gives her teams the footing they need to stretch, experiment, and move forward with confidence, especially when the terrain is new.

This is conviction in motion—a clear sense of identity guiding behavior, even under pressure. And it's the first turn of the Intentional Resilience flywheel.

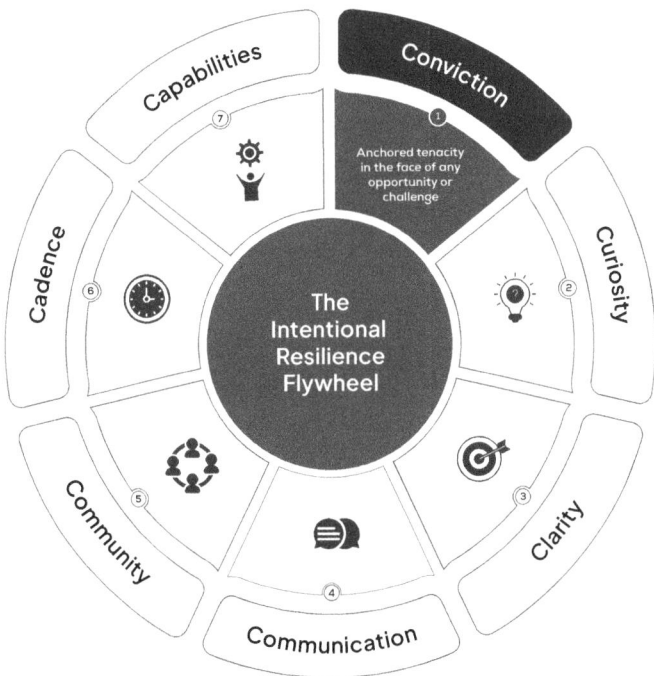

Trusting Your Gut

One of my CEO clients, who is smart, thoughtful, and well-resourced, came to an executive advisory coaching session completely burned out.

Arjun wasn't failing; he was over-functioning. Too many priorities. Too many yeses. Too much trying to be everything to everyone.

The stakes were high. Arjun runs a large organization with hundreds of millions of dollars of recurring revenue, and he needs to be "on" for his team so *they* can meet their deliverables and KPIs.

"I thought I was being productive," he said. "But I'm just running out of bandwidth."

We paused. We named what really mattered and then started subtracting. Arjun left that session with more focus. And that made all the difference in his energy. Peak performance doesn't mean saying yes to everything. In fact, it often means knowing what to say no to—and having the confidence to do so.

This topic brings us to the first flywheel component: Conviction, a strong belief based on values and purpose. When you have conviction, you know who you are and where you stand. It allows you to set priorities, lead with confidence, and trust yourself.

Your team has the reassurance of which "you" they are getting and what guideposts you'll use to lead and make critical decisions. This creates stability and reduces friction, cascading conviction out to the team level.

At the organizational level, conviction shows up in meetings where risks and opportunities are carefully considered, where decisions are made that align with core values (not quick profits), and where boundaries are set, fairly applied, and enforced consistently.

Without conviction, everything else can tilt. If you don't know what you believe—if you haven't named the principles you'll protect and the values you'll act from—then the winds of external pressure will start making your decisions for you.

You'll bend to urgency, to volume, and to trend. And it will be exhausting.

But when conviction is clear, you don't spin out every time the environment shifts. You have an internal anchor, and from that anchor, you can build clarity. You can create community, adjust cadence, communicate with care, stay curious, and activate real capabilities. (These are all components of the flywheel, which is why we started here!)

Conviction is the moment you stop waiting for someone else to take responsibility. You take it and make decisions. From there, everything else becomes possible.

That internal anchor—conviction—does more than guide decisions. It stabilizes the entire system, especially when the environment is shifting and answers are scarce.

Conviction isn't just useful in calm conditions—it becomes essential when things get uncertain. When the path forward is unclear and the pressure to react quickly is high, conviction is what keeps you from spinning. It gives you a center of gravity. It is the foundation of Intentional Resilience.

The Relationship Between Conviction and Uncertainty

The human brain doesn't like uncertainty. It treats it like danger, so we try to close the loops too fast. We crave steadiness, even when it's false.

That's why conviction matters. Because in uncertain moments, we need to know what's guiding us. What we're here for. What we won't compromise. What questions still matter, even when the answers aren't clear.

When leaders hold that center—when they say, "We're still figuring it out, but here's what doesn't change"—they don't eliminate the fear and uncertainty entirely, but they do shrink the chaos. They remind people that forward motion is still possible.

There's a cost to a lack of conviction, and it's not just internal. When you walk into some companies, everything feels transactional: tasks, metrics, and CYA meetings (a.k.a. Cover Your Ass). The problem is that no one remembers the "why," and the only goal is survival.

And then there are cultures where people have a sense of shared belief—not in a slogan, a catchy mission statement, or lofty values embossed on the lobby wall—but in an unspoken quality that feels real.

Over time, leadership conviction becomes a culture where people work together instead of staying huddled in silos, protecting their territory.

Conviction has many facets: confidence, self-awareness, thoughtfulness, risk tolerance, and the ability to make decisions. Intentionally Resilient leaders use their conviction like a beacon of light to cut through chaos.

Standing Strong When It Counts the Most

In the high-stakes world of leadership and innovation, conviction isn't just a desirable quality; it's a critical skill. For Oliver Albers, Head of Investment Intelligence at Nasdaq, conviction has been the foundation of his career, enabling him to navigate change, lead through uncertainty, and find balance in a demanding professional and personal life.

"Resilience is actually a muscle that you strengthen a little bit every day," Oliver explained. It's not a quality reserved for crises but a proactive approach to handling life's challenges. This mindset has shaped his ability to embrace change, maintain optimism, and continue growing both personally and professionally.

When Oliver was thirty-seven, he was diagnosed with lymphoma. That unexpected diagnosis sharpened his perspective and his commitment to his core values. After his recovery, he was more confident in taking professional risks. He's taken on increasingly challenging roles at Nasdaq because he is not afraid of failing. To Oliver, every experience is an opportunity to learn and position himself for additional growth.

Oliver sees a direct connection between conviction and innovation. "If you want the ball to bounce back up, you have to innovate," he explained. Conviction allows leaders and teams to approach challenges with a mindset of curiosity and problem-solving, rather than fear and resistance.

Making decisions requires confidence, information, and trust in your own ideas. A leader who lacks conviction waffles, avoids, and fails to act.

I once consulted with a company whose leadership team kept delaying a major organizational change. Everyone agreed it was necessary, but no one wanted to say it aloud. The CEO was well-liked, smart, and visionary. But he hesitated—again and again. The delay didn't buy him goodwill.

It bred confusion. People started second-guessing each other. The high performers left first, and the rest got stuck in analysis paralysis. By the time the changes were made, it was too late to shape the narrative around them.

Conviction isn't about moving fast; it's about moving with courage before the opportunity calcifies.

Conviction as Power

Ashley Black is a globally recognized entrepreneur. She is the founder of the Fascia Blaster, a bestselling author, and the leader of a movement that has helped millions reclaim their health through fascia therapy and self-healing. A medical survivor and self-taught fascia expert, Ashley transformed personal trauma into a wellness empire, built not on hype but on purpose.

Ashley doesn't sugarcoat her story. At age thirty, she contracted a rare bone infection that led to sepsis, organ shutdown, a coma, and the loss of part of her pelvis. "I wasn't near death. I died," she confided. While Ashley came back to life, she was not the same. She came back with a mission, determined to heal her own body and help others do the same. Her conviction would eventually become the foundation for a movement that changed how people think about fascia, health, and healing.

"I knew I had something to bring to the world. That's why I came back."

Ashley's calling gave her the determination to create a body of work and a global reach, despite copycats and a class-action lawsuit. When those attacks came, Ashley didn't spiral. She'd already done the inner work.

"You can't cancel someone who's complete. I had nothing to hide, no persona to uphold."

Instead of defending, she recalibrated and focused. And she kept showing up for her customers. "You want to win in business? Be so aligned with your purpose that you're not shook when people come for you."

Like Archana and Oliver, Ashley used her conviction to stand tall during times of uncertainty and profound stress. Our next story gives you a look behind the scenes at how another leader coped with the intensity of the COVID-19 pandemic, which disrupted her business model.

The Power of Naming What You Believe

Brandi Joplin is the former CFO of Sam's Club. The retail giant was profoundly impacted by the turbulence of the pandemic. Supply chains were massively disrupted, customer demand shifted significantly to curbside pickup and home delivery, and team members were battling burnout from uncertain personal situations. No one could predict what would happen next or when the situation would end.

Brandi shared that she learned to be brave enough to name what she believes to be true, even before she had a full answer. She would tell her team, "We may have to rewrite this plan again in a week. But here's where I'm anchored." By staying focused on each phase—having conviction in operational technology innovation and AI forecasting initiatives—Brandi oversaw a 40 percent increase in sales in a three-year period and achieved record membership growth.

That's what conviction does. It doesn't eliminate change. It helps people move through it.

Conviction doesn't require a full change-management plan. It requires the courage to stop pretending we're fine, the openness to ask better questions, and the willingness to move forward even when the picture feels incomplete.

That's what builds trust and forward motion. Our next example is from a leader who has the conviction to be comfortable with uncertainty—and even chaos—long before it arrives.

Courting Intelligent Risk

Chris Hoffmann is an SVP and Global Privacy Officer for Robert Half, a major professional services and staffing firm. His entire job focuses on risk. Yet he's made peace with it. That peace doesn't come from denial—it comes from preparation and practice.

At least once per year, Chris and his crisis team simulate a security and privacy incident: a ransomware attack, a rogue employee, a sudden system failure, or a mistakenly sent email. They write scenarios based on emerging threats, and they run the drill as if it were real, complete with CEO briefings, communication protocols, and postmortem reviews.

Why? So that when a real threat hits, it's not the first time anyone on his team has faced, discussed, or contemplated different types of security and privacy incidents.

"Preparation is the key to success," Chris said. "When you get anxious, your brain functions differently. You want and need the muscle memory already there so you can act decisively and without hesitation."

That proactive approach to risk is the bedrock of his team's culture. So much so that their department mantra is: "Be bold. Intelligent risks are essential for success." It's on their email signatures, it's baked into their decision-making, and it's a quality Chris tries to model personally as a leader.

He recalls a moment when a senior member of his team made a decision that didn't turn out well. But it was the right call given the information the leader had at the time. Chris didn't scold, and he didn't micromanage. He offered a quiet course correction and moved on. He's built psychological safety into his team so that mistakes aren't punished. "If you can justify your decision rationally, even if it's wrong, we're not going to get upset," he said. "But if you make a decision with no thought behind it, that's a different story."

That philosophy of intelligent risk-taking has helped his department avoid becoming the stereotypical "Department of No." Instead, they aim to be the *Partner of Yes*—a department that balances opportunity with accountability.

Chris knows that playing it safe isn't always the safest move. "Sometimes not doing something is a bigger risk than trying something bold," he said. "And if it fails? We'll figure it out."

What makes Chris's approach powerful is not just his tolerance for risk but his conviction in how to approach risks: thoughtfully, transparently, and with a willingness to own the outcome. That conviction, rooted in preparation, perspective, and a long view of success, is what makes his leadership noteworthy.

Summary

As you've seen, conviction appears in many forms. For some, it's in decisive action or confident decision-making. For others, it's in preparing teams for chaos so they are calm when it arrives. In all cases, conviction provides a foundation of confidence: When you are aligned with clear purpose and values, you take intelligent risks and optimize decisions, bolstering Intentional Resilience.

Conviction allows you to step forward into uncertainty with your eyes open, your team beside you, and a plan in your back pocket. Without conviction, your flywheel will waver and wobble, as will your team. Conviction gives you the courage to embrace the next component: Curiosity.

Micro-Steps

In the following chapters, we'll cover each of the seven components of the Intentional Resilience Flywheel. You'll be invited to take a few small steps to apply what you've discovered and enhance your muscle memory in each arena.

Conviction isn't about waiting until you're certain; it's about moving forward because your courage is strong. Consider the following ideas to assess your current level of conviction, then try small experiments to strengthen it.

Start here by reflecting:

- When was the last time you said "yes" to something risky—and meant it? How did you decide to say "yes"?
- Think back to a recent tough decision. Did you trust your instincts, your values, or the data most? Why?
- Are you modeling confident action for your team, or waiting for conditions to feel safer? Why?

Try these micro-steps:

- At your next team meeting, ask: "What are we doing because we believe in it, not just because it's expected?"
- Create a "decision log" this week. For each tough decision, jot down the inputs, your reasoning, and what value it reflects.
- Rehearse risk. Choose one project and run a "pre-mortem." What could go wrong? How would you respond? What support would you need? What previous situation does this resemble, and how can you apply learnings from that situation?

Conviction isn't about eliminating doubt. It's about choosing the best path, even when that path isn't perfectly lit. When you know who you are, you stand firm in your conviction. That stability is a key element of Intentional Resilience, and a serious business asset.

Now, let's turn to the next component on the flywheel: curiosity.

CHAPTER 5

CURIOSITY—THE SPARK OF INNOVATION

Curiosity is often framed as whimsical. It's seen as a personality trait or a bonus quality you hope your kids develop. But in the context of Intentional Resilience, curiosity is essential.

Curiosity turns pressure into insight. Without it, leaders default to what they already know. They get stuck in their existing maps, and they see obstacles instead of opportunities. But when curiosity is alive in a system, teams don't just survive change, they spark it.

That spark is why Intentionally Resilient organizations make space for questions. They don't wait for a crisis to unlock creativity. They teach people to shift from asking, "What went wrong?" to, "What's possible?"

I once worked with an organization in the middle of a major leadership transition. Morale was shaky, and the economy was uncertain. They invited me in to facilitate a session on navigating ambiguity.

I told them, "Great. We're going to talk about curiosity as a tool."

And the company's HR leader said, "We don't have processes for curiosity, so let's leave that off your workshop."

My jaw dropped. (Spoiler alert: That company is still struggling. I'm not surprised.)

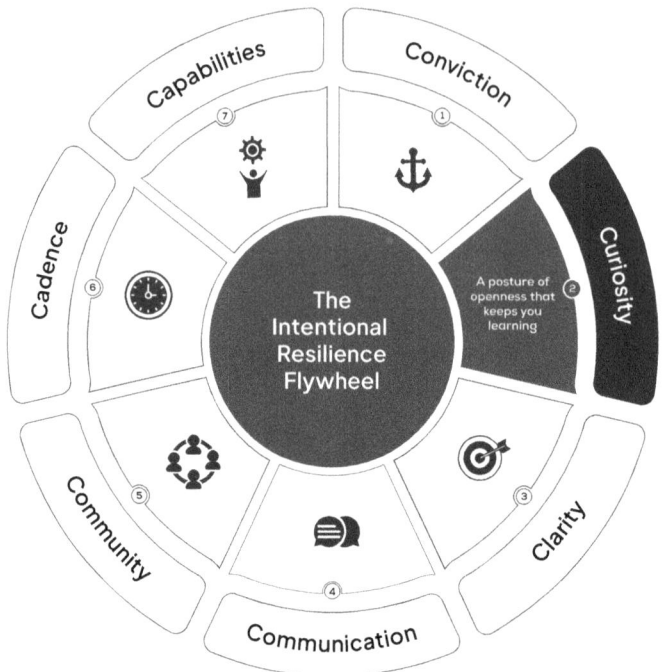

Curiosity as a Strategic Lever

At The Campbell's Company (formerly Campbell Soup Company), where Julia Anderson most recently served as Chief Technology and Information Officer, the company's values include five core C's: Caring, Character, Collaboration, Competitiveness, and Community. But ask Julia what she sees as essential to building an innovative team, and she'll tell you there's a sixth C: Curiosity.

"Without curiosity," she said, "you're not living to the full potential of what you can do in your role."

For Julia, curiosity isn't a soft trait; it's a strategic lever. It's how innovation happens, how transformation takes root, and how Intentional Resilience gets hardwired into the organization. She saw it firsthand.

In one of her early transformations at Campbell's, Julia noticed a frustrating pattern: a culture of waiting. Teams hesitated to propose innovative ideas. People defaulted to what was already working, even if it wasn't working well. Many felt that they needed permission to challenge the status quo.

So, Julia removed that barrier. She launched hackathons and innovation sprints. She gave teams dedicated "grow time" to explore their ideas, whether that meant experimenting with AI to automate routine approvals or building tools to eliminate unnecessary spreadsheets. She created a visible, celebrated space where people could bring forward pain points, solve them, and share success stories across the company.

"Curiosity and permission," she said, "unlock possibility. You don't need to wait to be told what's broken. If you're curious, you'll find it. And if you're empowered, you'll fix it."

Her leadership model rewired how Campbell's thought about change. Projects no longer had to be top-down or tied to massive timelines and budgets. If employees saw a problem, such as an outdated manual process, a data lag, or a clunky user experience, they were encouraged to solve it. And they were celebrated for it.

That cultural shift opened the floodgates. Before this curiosity initiative, Julia's division tackled three to five big projects each year. After Julia embedded curiosity, they took on more than seventy projects, each one with personal ownership. Teams weren't overwhelmed. Instead, they were engaged because the ideas came from them. The outcomes weren't just incremental improvements. They were catalysts for entirely new ways of working.

Julia doesn't credit this change to a formal transformation framework but to a more human quality: the decision to be endlessly curious.

When asked how curiosity fuels Intentional Resilience, Julia doesn't hesitate. "Curious people don't panic when things break," she said. "They get excited. They ask better questions. They move faster. And they bring others with them."

That's why her team spotlighted failures as much as wins during weekly portfolio reviews. They focused on lessons rather than assigning blame. And they invited others to learn from those mistakes—while continuing to learn themselves.

For Julia, innovation doesn't start with a budget or a blueprint. It starts with a question.

Culture Change Starts with Noticing

Curiosity is not just about what you *ask*. It's about what you *see*.

Remember Charles Newnam from Chapter 2? He's the former submarine officer who moved a tiny plastic submarine one stop at a time in the ship's control room to help his crew see measurable forward movement in the long, tedious months serving underwater. Today, Charles is a Principal Director at Accenture.

Charles employed curiosity as a driver for thoughtful change with a quiet first step: helping people learn how to notice.

He found that in a controlled environment like a submarine, it could be easy to slip into routines and disengage curiosity. So, he encouraged his submarine crew to:

- Notice what is working.
- Notice what is frustrating.
- Notice how behavior is landing.
- Notice who seems pressured.
- Notice where time is wasted.

Charles took this practice into his consulting work, where he encourages curiosity by conducting five-minute micro-experiments. These experiments are tiny acts of doing things differently, such as shaking up the meeting agenda, changing the question format, skipping the slide deck, or letting someone else lead the meeting.

If a new approach works, do it again. If not, no harm. But learning will always occur. He credits these small moments with creating big—and sometimes unexpected—outcomes.

This is how curiosity scales—through safe, visible, and repeatable actions.

Curiosity Drives Growth

In some companies, curiosity is treated as a luxury, something to explore when the timeline is generous, when the budget allows, or when the dust settles.

But the most Intentionally Resilient leaders don't wait for room, they make it.

Karen Stuckey is a former Senior Vice President at Walmart, where she led a $40 billion-plus general merchandise Private Brand discipline encompassing home goods, apparel, hardware, stationery, sporting goods, automotive, electronics, and seasonal products.

When Karen was pulled out of a high-performing, high-visibility merchandising role and reassigned to a struggling business unit in which four executives had already rotated through, it could have been demoralizing. She had just earned the title of Merchandising SVP of the Year, and she'd uprooted her family to move cross-country for the job. Now, she was being placed in a role no one wanted—one defined more by turnover than triumph.

But Karen didn't approach it as a demotion; she approached it as a blank page.

"If this were a brand-new business," she asked herself, "what would I do from scratch?"

That single question changed everything.

Rather than trying to replicate what hadn't worked, Karen leaned into her curiosity. She asked questions no one else had paused to ask, such as: Why do merchants hate this process? Why haven't the previous strategies stuck? What if we stopped treating this like a plug-and-play business unit and started over with fresh assumptions?

She built a strategy from the ground up—a new structure, new systems, and new communication loops. She didn't make assumptions based on legacy processes. Instead, she tested everything.

Before she brought any of it to leadership, she went to her peers and stakeholders—the merchants, the sourcing teams, and the product developers—and floated her ideas. She wanted buy-in, not just sign-off.

"Curiosity gave me the freedom to reimagine the role," she said. "No one else knew this business the way I would. And because no one expected it to succeed, I had the space to try something radically different."

That curiosity paid off. Karen turned the struggling unit into a growth engine. She was given more responsibility—product development, technical and creative design, quality, sourcing, and brand management, leading this brand-new discipline she had grown. She even ended up mentoring the executive who had been placed in her previous role.

Karen doesn't tell this story as a victory lap. She shares it as a case study in how curiosity fuels innovation.

"When you treat ambiguity as a starting point, not a threat, you unlock possibility," she said. "People freeze in uncertainty because they're afraid of being wrong. But if no one knows the answer yet, why not be the one who figures it out?"

Karen encouraged this mindset in her teams, too. In strategy sessions, she ran "what if" drills: What are all the things that could go wrong? What risks haven't we considered? What new moves would we make if we weren't constrained by history?

This wasn't idle speculation; it was scenario-planning, a curiosity-powered form of building Intentional Resilience. When the unexpected happened—as it always does—her team didn't freeze. They'd already rehearsed mentally, so they could keep moving.

Curiosity fuels agility. When you question assumptions early, you reduce rework later.

What If We Looked at This Differently?

Luca Fioravanti brings curiosity into every endeavor. As Group Head of Security for Dolce & Gabbana, and with decades of cross-industry leadership including telecom, finance, and luxury goods, Luca is no stranger to navigating complex change, high-stakes environments, and unpredictable risk.

Years ago, when Luca worked in the telecom industry during a major business outage that wasn't his company's fault, the easy play would have been to pass the blame. But his CEO chose a different path—offering replacement devices and increased support to affected clients, transforming a technical crisis into a business opportunity. That move didn't come from panic or pressure. It came from curiosity: *What if we looked at this differently? What if we turned this into trust with our customers?*

Luca never forgot that.

Today, curiosity is part of how he leads, mentors, and grows teams. He encourages his staff—not just his senior leaders, but junior colleagues and interns as well—to ask questions before jumping to the answers, to dig into assumptions, and to sit with uncertainty long enough to uncover possibilities.

"Curiosity helps you see what's possible and also what's dangerous. It prepares you to act wisely, not impulsively."

Even at home, this philosophy carries over. When mentoring his daughter, Luca doesn't give direct advice. He shares stories instead, encouraging her to explore and weigh her choices through her own lens. "The most valuable tool I can give her is the ability to be curious. To listen deeply. Then she'll know what to do."

In Luca's world, curiosity is not a trait reserved for the young or the idealistic. It is a discipline, a habit that keeps leaders agile and grounded at the same time. It's how innovation begins—not with the pressure to be original but with the humility to ask, "What else might be true?"

Getting Curious About Failure

Most people aren't afraid of failing. They are afraid of what happens after. They're afraid of being humiliated, sidelined, slowed down, or shut out. So, they wait. They hedge. They try to perfect the plan instead of testing it early. But I've learned that Intentionally Resilient organizations don't punish failure, they mine it. They move through it and turn mistakes into momentum by shifting the story from defeat to data.

Failure, for me, is different from defeat. Failure is information. Defeat is judgment. When leaders know the difference—and model that difference—teams get braver. They get faster. More creative. More resilient.

The best way to make failure less scary for your team is to share your own—not the neat version, but the real one. To say, "Here's where I missed it. Here's what I learned. Here's what we'll do differently now."

I call it the twelve-degree pivot. Most problems don't require a full reinvention; they just need a new angle. Something didn't work? Adjust it, reapply it, and let learning do its job.

That's what I practiced in my own software company. Trust didn't rise when everything went right. Trust rose when something went wrong and no one got punished for it. We wouldn't have survived if I had shut people down every time we hit friction. What built our momentum was the feeling that you could miss the mark and still move forward. That's what makes people brave.

That kind of safety isn't soft, it's strategic. In Intentionally Resilient teams, failure is the first step in what we build next.

Summary

Curiosity has a direct link to innovation, growth, and process improvement. When leaders are brave enough to ask questions and to give their teams permission to question and explore, morale increases and discoveries accelerate.

Curiosity requires conviction. Leaders who are tied to the status quo or mired in policies and procedures are often masking a fear of change. Intentionally Resilient leaders welcome innovative ideas with courage.

They ask questions like:

- What friction could we remove today?
- If we had the budget and resources, what would we build?
- What data are we sitting on that we've never actually looked at?
- What did we learn from our latest failure?
- What do our customers wish we would stop (or start) doing?

These are not rhetorical questions. They are invitations. Curiosity becomes Intentional Resilience when it opens a door, not just to novelty but to wisdom.

Leaders can bring curiosity to their teams in small ways, such as lunch and learns, Friday brainstorms, walking meetings, idea walls, or a rotating host for weekly check-ins. The signal is this: Your ideas are welcome here, even if they are rough—*especially* if they are rough.

The opposite of curiosity is not ignorance but resignation. And resignation is the old, reactive model of resilience that says, "something will happen *to* me." But with the lens of curiosity, you can powerfully shift to the Intentional Resilience model and ask: "What growth, innovation, or competitive advantage can happen *through* me?"

Micro-Steps

Curiosity doesn't have to mean grand experiments or overnight reinvention. It starts with what you notice, what you're willing to ask, and what you're brave enough to rethink. It means staying available to possibilities, even when the path ahead is unclear. The most Intentionally Resilient cultures don't just allow questions—they reward them.

How comfortable are you with curiosity?

Start here by reflecting:

- What's one process, meeting, or habit in your team that you've accepted, but haven't questioned?
- What's a problem that your team keeps tolerating instead of tackling?
- When was the last time you asked someone, "What do you wish we'd stop doing?"

Try these micro-steps:

- Begin your next team meeting with a curiosity round: What are you seeing? What's not working? What are you wondering about?
- Pick one system you use daily—an approval form, a report, or a workflow—and ask: Why do we do it this way?
- Host a "what if" session. No slides, just questions. One focused hour of open thinking.

You don't need permission to be curious. You need practice, and the more you practice it, the more Intentionally Resilient you and your organization will become. Plus, asking all those questions leads you to the next component on the flywheel: clarity.

CHAPTER 6

CLARITY—THE FOUNDATION OF DECISION-MAKING

When Doug Peterson was the Chief Auditor of Citigroup, he was sent to Japan to fix a regulatory crisis. He walked into a storm. Two of the firm's businesses, a trust bank and a private bank, were under heavy scrutiny. Serious lapses had occurred in how clients were treated. Regulators were angry, and employees were scared. Morale had tanked, and the culture was on the edge of collapse.

Doug wasn't there to patch it up. He was there to lead through it. And he knew that meant doing more than damage control.

His first move was to do what he now calls "ring-fencing." He identified the heart of the crisis and contained it, along with a team of dedicated experts. Then, he made a bold promise to the rest of the organization: "This is not your problem to carry."

"I told them, 'You don't need to panic. We're fixing this. We've got our best people on it. If we need your help, we'll ask. Otherwise, keep doing your work. Keep serving our clients. We'll keep you informed every step of the way.'"

That move changed everything. The fear began to settle, and people started breathing again. They could do their jobs without looking over their shoulders. They had permission to focus forward.

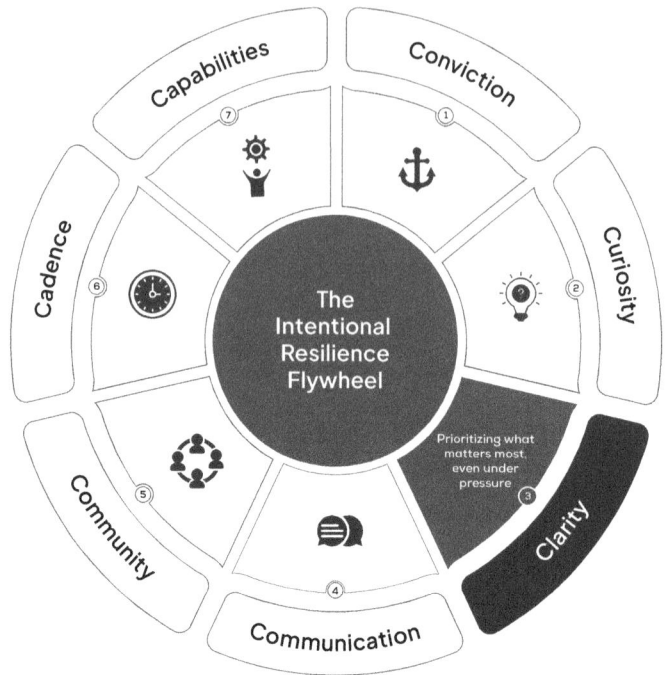

Project Kei

Then Doug did something even more powerful.

While a team of experts tackled the crisis, he pulled together a group of about twenty-five high-potential employees from across the organization. He called it Project Kei, named after the Japanese word for "respect." These weren't just trusted lieutenants. They were diverse, cross-functional voices from every corner of the company, including marketing, compliance, finance, operations, and customer service.

Their mission? Rebuild the future of Citigroup in Japan.

Doug didn't want to just fix what was broken. He wanted to transform how the business showed up, both internally and externally. He challenged the Project Kei team to rethink the business from the ground up. What would it take not only to regain trust but to earn new levels of respect in the market? What could the new model of a financial franchise in Japan look like?

This wasn't a branding exercise. It was a culture reset.

Doug's combination of ring-fencing the crisis and investing in a future-facing team created something rare: calm in the middle of a storm, and belief in a better future.

"I learned to do both at once," he said. "Stabilize the crisis and simultaneously design what comes next."

He took that same approach years later as CEO of McGraw-Hill—later to become S&P Global. When McGraw-Hill faced massive litigation from the Department of Justice and multiple state attorneys general, he used the same playbook: ring-fence the legal battles, communicate clearly, and free up the rest of the organization to move forward with confidence.

His goal wasn't just containment. It was a restoration of clarity.

Space for Deciding

Clarity, for Doug, is not about oversimplifying complex situations. It's about creating the emotional and operational space to make smart decisions. Sometimes, that clarity requires a dispassionate objectivity that most leaders struggle to find in the heat of a crisis.

"I'm not a 'hair-on-fire' kind of guy," he said. "In crisis, I stay calm. I look for what's actually true. What can we act on? What matters most right now?"

That calm presence, paired with intentional structure, becomes a resilience strategy all its own. Doug doesn't tell people to "just get back on the horse." He gives them a hand up. He creates a plan. He lets them know they won't be thrown off again.

That's why people followed him—not just through crisis but through change.

Doug's story is a masterclass in clarity-driven Intentional Resilience. He doesn't sugarcoat the challenge. He doesn't ask his teams to pretend everything's fine. He also doesn't let fear lead. He gives people enough structure to feel safe, enough vision to feel inspired, and enough transparency to stay engaged.

And it works. The crisis in Japan was resolved, the brand regained strength, and the team, many of whom had felt ashamed, paralyzed, or uncertain, found new pride in their work. They went beyond surviving the storm and helped rebuild the future.

The Leadership Calm That Powers Intentional Resilience

Clarity isn't just a communication tactic; it's an Intentional Resilience strategy.

Over the years, through coaching hundreds of senior leaders and guiding teams through constant transformation, I've learned that the most Intentionally Resilient organizations are not necessarily the ones with the best tools or the boldest ideas. They are the ones where people know where they're going, what matters, and how to make aligned decisions, even when everything around them is shifting.

When there's too much ambiguity, people freeze or burn out. Not because they're fragile but because they're paddling hard in different directions, unsure of what success looks like. It's exhausting. That's where burnout hides—not in the amount of work but in the lack of direction.

Our job as leaders is not to create certainty where there is none. It's to reduce unnecessary uncertainty wherever we can.

Closing Pockets of Uncertainty

At Relativity Space, Kim Nakamaru, whom you met in Chapter 3, doesn't just lead with strategy; she prioritizes clarity. One of Kim's most consistent leadership practices is what she calls "closing pockets of uncertainty."

"When you're leading during change," she told me, "you won't have all the answers. But you do have the power to reduce ambiguity."

In team meetings, she names the uncertainty directly: "This is the part I can't share yet. This is the part I don't know. But here's what I *do* know. Here's what I can promise." That kind of transparency doesn't just inform people, it calms them.

"I believe most people can handle uncertainty," she said. "What they can't handle is unknowns with no leadership response. The more you help people focus on what's still true, the more they stay engaged."

Kim doesn't fill the silence with spin. She doesn't fake optimism. She aims to create the cognitive space for teams to make decisions, act, and move forward, even in imperfect circumstances.

It's not just a corporate tactic, as Kim and her husband use the same approach at home. They sit down regularly to evaluate their family values and priorities *before* the pressure builds. That alignment helps her make tough choices with clarity, both personally and professionally.

"We don't wait for chaos to have the conversation," she told me. "We close the gaps early."

That habit is one of the most underrated forms of Intentional Resilience: helping others move forward by reducing the swirl. Even when you can't fix the storm, you can still guide people toward steadiness.

How Intentionally Resilient Leaders Create Clarity:

- State your values and lead according to those values.
- Prioritize what matters now.
- Name what's unknown, and anchor it in what you *do* know.
- Ring-fence a crisis.
- Focus on what you can control.

Values Are Your Compass, Not a Poster in the Lobby

Clarity starts with values—but not the ones in the employee handbook or on the lobby wall at the company headquarters. I'm talking about real values, lived values—the kind you lead with on the ground.

I advise leaders to identify their top three values and explain why they matter, how they show up in their behavior, and what outcomes they're meant to drive.

Take my own top three values: transparency, respect, and integrity.

Transparency means I'll tell you what I know, as soon as I can share it, because people deserve to make decisions for themselves and their families. Respect means no yelling, no bullying, and no ambiguity in how we treat each other. Integrity means doing the right thing, even when it's hard.

When I was leading my software startup, these values helped me make hard decisions. For example, some investors prefer that startup CEOs keep quiet about their company's financial runway. They believe it can be distracting to employees to be aware of the financial turbulence of early-stage startups. But that idea is in direct conflict with my values of transparency and respect. My team deserved the truth. So, I told them. That gave them power and clarity. It gave them a choice.

That's what values do when they're real. They don't just decorate the wall—they guide the hardest decisions.

Making Hard Choices Easier

The moments that test us the most don't happen in boardrooms. They happen in the real world—in our families, in our private crises, and in the decisions no one else sees.

Darin Wolter, the Chief Revenue Officer at Specright and a longtime startup executive, told me a story I can't stop thinking about. It wasn't about a sales target or a leadership pivot. It was about his mom.

Several years ago, Darin's mother experienced a sudden and catastrophic decline due to dementia. What had once been a slow, expected progression accelerated into a four-month freefall. The family had to make an unthinkable decision: to move her into memory care as quickly as possible.

Darin didn't start the decision-making process with the logistics. He started with values.

He and his siblings toured multiple facilities. Most touted their amenities, and a few prioritized their clinical expertise. But only one led the conversation with something else: a clear, deeply held set of values.

"They could articulate who they were," Darin said. "How they treated their staff. How they showed up for their residents. And how they sustained themselves emotionally in this demanding work."

That clarity made the decision easier. Not cheaper, not more convenient, but right.

When Darin described the situation to me, I could feel how deeply the lesson landed: "I learned that from work," he said. "From leading through tough calls. From knowing that when values are clear, everything else gets simpler."

I've seen the same truth play out in business repeatedly. It's easy to proclaim your company values on the website. It's a lot harder for leaders and teams to navigate by a clear set of true, lived leadership values. Without this, every choice is harder. Priorities blur, people burn out, and teams spin. But when you lead with values and embed them in your decisions, they become your ballast. They keep you upright when the winds pick up.

Darin knows this firsthand. His own leadership values—fairness, hard and smart work, customer-first focus, and growth—aren't just theoretical. They shape how he structures deals, builds culture, and trains new hires. During every onboarding session, he shares the same message: "When you don't know what to do next, go back to your values. They will guide you."

Whether you're choosing a memory care home for a loved one or deciding which client to serve, the principle holds: clarity in values creates clarity in action. What works at home, works in organizations, too, because clarity isn't dependent on context: it's human.

That's why I say that Intentional Resilience starts long before a challenge or a crisis. It begins with knowing who you are, what you stand for, and how you—and your values—show up when the stakes are real.

Why Clarity Reduces Burnout and Increases Confidence

Clarity on the Intentional Resilience flywheel is about more than values. It's also about setting and securing alignment about what work everyone is doing together, and why.

I've seen it repeatedly: When people understand the direction, they find their own energy. When they understand why a decision was made—even if they don't agree with it—they stay in the game. That clarity is what keeps people engaged, and it's what creates alignment, momentum, and emotional headspace.

Too often, though, I walk into companies where the leadership team has just given a big, rousing keynote ... and the audience walks away with twenty-five different takeaways. I do a quick exercise: I ask them to write down the three most important points they've just heard. If I get twenty-five different answers, we have a clarity problem, and it's unlikely the team will meet that quarter's objectives.

Clarity means your people can answer three questions:

- What is the most important outcome?
- What do we need to do to achieve that outcome?
- What's my role in getting us there?

If they can answer those, even in a turbulent environment, they'll move—and move fast. They'll stretch. They'll innovate. And they won't waste energy second-guessing what's expected.

Prioritization: Clarity in Motion

Priorities are where clarity gets tested. It's not enough to know your values. You need to know what you're here to do—and how that translates into the choices you make daily.

We're often told that "no" is a complete sentence. But when you explain that "no" through the lens of priority—what you were hired to do, what your team needs most, and what the current moment demands—it becomes more powerful.

When you're clear on your top three responsibilities, it becomes easier to triage and easier to say, "I was brought in to deliver these outcomes. I don't bring my greatest value when I step outside of that lane."

It's not deflection, it's focus.

The Cost of Friction

One of the most honest definitions of burnout I've heard didn't come from a wellness doctor or a research paper. It came from Dr. Kim Abrego, the Chief Operating Officer of Disaster Recovery Services, a disaster response firm that handles billion-dollar recovery efforts for government and private sector clients across the USA.

"Burnout," she told me, "isn't too much work. It's too much friction."

Friction, in her experience, comes from one thing: unclear priorities. That's why Kim leads differently. She leads with radical consistency, with modeled permission, and always, always with values as her compass.

Kim travels a lot. Last year, she was on the road for 180 days in dozens of short, high-intensity trips. She's a mother, a competitive bodybuilder, and the operational heart of a company that's scaling fast while navigating change. And yet, she maintains her focus by doing the right things consistently.

That's her mantra: consistency over intensity.

"I didn't compete this year," she said, referring to her usual bodybuilding competitions. "I couldn't. The travel was too much. But I still trained. Maybe it wasn't leg presses and stage prep, but it was walking on the hotel treadmill. Eating well. Moving my body. I don't miss two days in a row. That's my rule."

What I love about Kim's approach is that it isn't about chasing balance. In fact, she calls out that myth directly.

"Balance is bullshit," she told me, laughing. "Life comes in seasons. You can't do everything all the time. But you can do the most important thing right now, and do it with clarity."

That's where prioritization comes in, not as a to-do list but as an act of cognitive kindness. Kim doesn't ask her team to juggle everything at once. When the company launched a sales initiative with five thousand warm leads to contact, she didn't frame it as a mountain. She broke it down into daily, repeatable chunks.

"We went from panic to progress," she said. "And because it was manageable, people didn't freeze. They moved."

This description is what Intentionally Resilient leadership looks like in real life. It's what you model every day.

Kim does that in a dozen small ways. She blocks her calendar for workouts, email resets, and breaks. She doesn't hide those blocks but instead makes them visible so her team knows it's okay to do the same. She's learned that people don't believe what you *say* about boundaries; they believe what you *model*.

"I use my values as a compass," she said. "They help me decide. Do I take this new opportunity, or say no? Do I push forward, or pause? If it's not a hell yes, and if it doesn't align with those values, it's a no."

Recently, after completing a major leadership fellowship, Kim was offered a spot in another high-prestige program. On paper, it was a dream opportunity, but when she looked at her values, the answer was clear.

"I'd just finished a season of learning and leading," she said. "Now I needed a season of being home. Being satisfied." And so, she said no—with zero regret. She wasn't choosing less. She was choosing alignment.

That's the power of clarity: the freedom to focus, the confidence to pause, and the energy to keep going when it matters most.

Fighting Today's Fire

Sometimes, Intentional Resilience looks like laser focus, and sometimes, it looks like letting go. While they might look different, they're actually two sides of the same coin.

Gwen Shaneyfelt, the Chief Administrative Officer of global investment management firm Franklin Templeton, navigates massive tax and regulatory environments every day. She doesn't try to fix every problem at once or drown in competing crises. Instead, she puts them in a box. Literally.

"When there's a challenge," she told me, "but it's not the right time to address it, I put it in a mental box and wall it off. It's not that I forget about it. I just know today isn't the day to solve it."

For Gwen, it's about discipline rather than avoidance. She's clear on what needs her energy now and what doesn't. With responsibilities spanning dozens of countries and functions, she's learned that Intentional Resilience means knowing what can wait.

Gwen's box is never invisible. "If that issue explodes out of the box, I deal with it," she said. "But I don't let it consume my day if it's not today's fire."

This isn't just operational triage. It's values-based leadership and pure clarity. Gwen protects what she cares about—her team, her integrity, and her energy—by saying no to the noise. And she teaches her people to do the same.

Not every storm is yours to chase. Some just need to stay in the box.

The Circle of Control

One of the most useful clarity tools I teach is the "circle of control." It's especially grounding for leaders and teams in functions where volatility is constant, like supply chain management.

We list what's in our control, such as relationships, pricing strategy, team morale, and communication cadence.

Then we list what's not in our control, such as geopolitics, inflation, tariffs, and global disruptions.

We look at the KPIs we're expected to deliver, and we build strategies from what's in our hands, not what's out of reach.

It's visual and simple. When leaders walk their teams through it, even during economic uncertainty or market disruption, it shifts the tone from helplessness to focus. This practice helps leaders create space in their own heads and space for their teams. I've used it myself in moments of overload. I ask, "What's in my control?" "What needs to be boxed for later?" (Thanks, Gwen!) "Where do I bring the most value?"

Asking yourself those clarifying questions can unlock calm, and from that calm, Intentional Resilience grows.

Summary

Clarity is not a luxury; it's a necessity. It reduces burnout, improves decision-making, and restores energy to leaders and teams. It means fewer misaligned yeses. Fewer wasted pivots. And more momentum.

Leaders who create clarity don't simplify reality. They make room for Intentional Resilience. They let people know what matters, give them space to act, and lead not by force—but by focus.

Micro-Steps

Clarity isn't about knowing everything. It's about knowing what matters *now*.

Start here by reflecting:

- What's one priority you've taken on that no longer aligns with your role or goals?
- Do all your team members know what initiatives will be the next focus?
- Which of your values have you used to make a decision this month?

Try these micro-steps:

- Write down your top three leadership values. Share one in your next team meeting and explain how it shapes your decisions.
- Block out thirty minutes to list your top three current priorities. Then cross-check your calendar. Are they showing up in where you're spending your time?
- Use the "circle of control" tool: On one side, list what you can influence. On the other side, list what you cannot control. Design your next steps based on what's yours to act on.

Clarity doesn't eliminate uncertainty. It reduces the noise so you can hear what matters. It gives you the ability to be heard because it sharpens your communication, which is the next turn on the flywheel.

CHAPTER 7

COMMUNICATION—THE LIFELINE OF INTENTIONAL RESILIENCE

Communication is one of the most underestimated drivers of Intentional Resilience. In challenging times, most organizations default to safe, tried-and-true strategies. (Remember the old saying, "No one was ever fired for buying IBM"?) But what companies really need in the face of disruption, what will sustain their positive momentum, is clear communication.

Without it, people fill in the gaps. Anxiety grows as teams assume the worst. Even the strongest teams start to fragment when they don't know what's coming, why it matters, or how they're supposed to respond.

Communication isn't just a skill set; it's a leadership discipline. And in Intentionally Resilient organizations, it's essential.

Cognitive Kindness

Cognitive kindness is the practice of being as clear as possible when you communicate. This practice removes the unnecessary workload on your listeners, who would otherwise have to unpack and interpret what you are saying. It means being clear instead of being vague, being transparent instead of hiding behind complexity, and giving context instead of issuing commands.

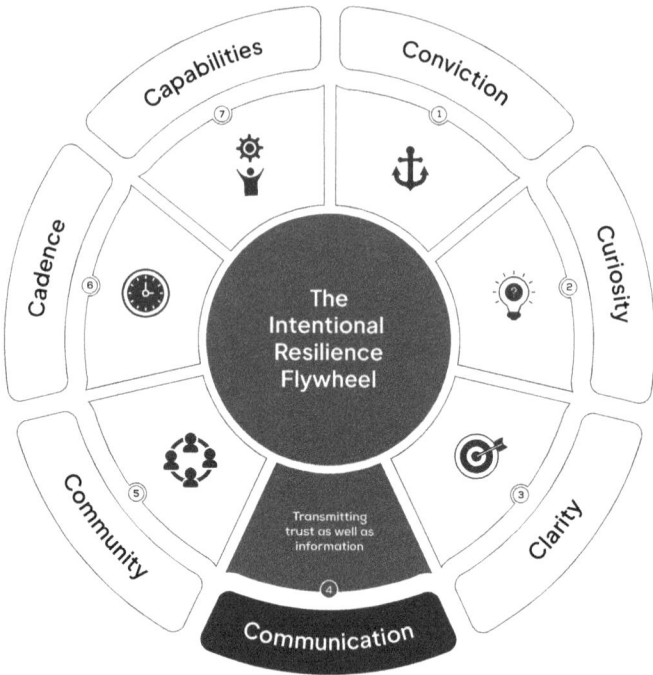

Cognitive kindness is a form of respect. When we communicate clearly, we offer relief from ambiguity. We give people the ability to focus, contribute, and recover faster. We stop making them guess what we mean or worry about what we're not saying.

This kind of clear communication does more than just transfer information. It builds trust and safety, and gives people the confidence to move, adapt, and lead—even when the path ahead isn't fully mapped out.

That's the work of Intentionally Resilient communication. In this chapter, we'll look at what it takes to do it well, from anchoring teams during change to choosing which narratives to amplify.

One of the clearest examples I've seen of communication as cognitive kindness comes from Julia Anderson, whom you met in Chapter 5. When Julia served as the Chief Technology and Information Officer at The Campbell's Company, she faced a challenge familiar to many modern leaders: how to guide a legacy organization through a massive digital transformation without losing the trust of its people.

Instead of treating communication as a one-way delivery system, she used it as a connective force to anchor, listen, and reframe. To invite people into the change rather than just announcing it.

Communication can feel abstract until you're in the middle of a challenge that demands it. For Julia, that moment came during the pandemic, when clarity, connection, and context were essential components of communication.

Connected Campbell's

Julia was at the helm of Campbell's technology organization during one of its most pivotal transitions. When the world shut down in 2020, the demand for shelf-stable food skyrocketed, and the Campbell's team had to pivot almost overnight. But the real challenge was as emotional as it was operational.

People were scared, burned out, and hungry for information. And that's where Julia stepped in. "We started something called Connected Campbell's," she explained. "It was our way of keeping people informed and grounded."

The format was simple: regular live-streamed updates that mixed business metrics with personal stories, leader spotlights, and moments of gratitude. Julia contextualized the numbers, named the challenges, and reminded her team of the bigger mission.

"It wasn't about putting a spin on things," she said. "It was about being real. And helping people feel part of something, even when we were apart."

When misinformation started to spread during a particularly stressful phase, Julia doubled down. "Silence creates stories," she said. "And not the good kind. If you don't close the gaps, people will fill them in with fear."

So, she got ahead of it. She shared what she knew, admitted what she didn't, and made sure her team never had to guess where the company stood—or where its decisions left them.

The result? A workforce that felt not just *informed*—but *trusted* with the truth, and a culture that treated communication not as a task, but as a leadership tool.

Communication during the pandemic was particularly challenging. Imagine if you were leading a group far out to sea during that time.

A Steady Voice in Stormy Seas

When COVID-19 began affecting Navy operations, Captain JJ Cummings knew uncertainty was the real enemy. As commander of the USS *Gerald R. Ford*—one of the largest aircraft carriers ever built—he led more than 2,700 sailors, each with family and fears beyond the ship.

He turned to his most consistent tool: communication. JJ delivered daily updates about the pandemic to the crew, even when there was no new information. His goal wasn't just to inform, but to anchor. "I'd rather be repetitive than silent," he said. His messages offered transparency, reassurance, and a steady hand in the storm.

"I didn't sugarcoat the situation," he recalled, "but I also reminded them of our mission. We were still moving forward—together."

This cadence of communication became a lifeline. Crew members began writing home about their captain's briefings. Parents emailed the Navy with thanks. Morale stayed remarkably high—not because conditions were easy, but because the steady communication reminded the team that no one was alone.

The lesson that JJ reinforced was to speak early, speak clearly, and speak with humanity.

Communication as an Accelerator for Change

Change is hard, and confusion makes it harder.

That's why communication is a driver, not just a support function, during transformation. A well-timed message can shift resistance into curiosity. A clear explanation can turn hesitation into action. And a thoughtful narrative can realign a team that's drifting into fear or fatigue.

Most leaders focus on what needs to change, but the most effective ones also pay attention to how people are experiencing that change and how their communication can help them reframe that experience in real time.

I call this "narrative-driven leadership." Not in the sense of spin but in the sense of intentionally shaping the meaning people take from a moment. Every change comes with multiple potential stories. Is this a story of loss or growth? Threat or opportunity? Disruption or evolution? We can't always control what's happening, but we can influence the interpretation.

Communication involves shaping the emotional architecture around a change, and it sets the tone for how people metabolize uncertainty. When we do it well, it speeds up clarity, trust, and alignment.

Please understand that acceleration doesn't mean rushing. It means helping people move with understanding, instead of forcing them to act before they're ready.

When I coach leaders through big transitions, I often ask them three simple questions:

- What is the story you're telling yourself about this moment?
- What is the story your team is likely telling themselves?
- What story do you need to build together to move forward?

That's not spin. It's care. It's communication as leadership. And it makes organizations more adaptable, more honest, and more Intentionally Resilient.

Our next story highlights that you can rarely overcommunicate.

Say It Until It's Boring

Marcus Grindstaff knows what it takes to build Intentionally Resilient teams because he's led them across startups, global medical device companies, and even high school robotics. At every level, his core belief is the same: You can't communicate too much when the stakes are high.

"If your team isn't a little tired of hearing your message," he said, "you probably haven't said it enough."

For Marcus, repetition isn't laziness. It's leadership. He sees communication as a way to reinforce clarity and build stability. In fast-moving environments, teams can't afford mixed messages or shifting explanations. What they need is consistency, predictability, and a shared rhythm of what matters and why.

In his words, "When the leader keeps saying the same thing—calmly, clearly, and consistently—it grounds the team. It tells them we're not flailing. We're focused."

Even in moments of change, Marcus resists the urge to reinvent the narrative. Instead, he reinforces it. His approach is simple: Say what's true. Say it clearly. Then say it again.

It might not sound exciting, but when people are stressed or stretched thin, clarity is a gift. And repetition is one of the most powerful tools of an Intentionally Resilient leader.

When the message is unpopular, clear communication is even more crucial.

Your Salary May Be Reduced

You met Elissar Farah Antonios in Chapter 2, where we explored the power of conviction during crisis. One of her most enduring leadership tools is her precise communication, especially in the moments when it would be easier to say less.

During a particularly turbulent financial period, Elissar had to make a difficult call: prepare her team for potential salary reductions. Some leaders would have delayed the conversation, softened it, or delegated it altogether. Elissar did the opposite.

She gathered her leadership team and spoke plainly. She explained the broader financial context and walked them through the data. Then she made it clear: no final decisions had been made, but the possibility of salary cuts was real—and she wanted her team to be part of the solution.

It wasn't easy, but it was honest. And it worked.

By giving her team the full picture, she didn't just deliver information—she invited ownership. That conversation, she said, built more trust than almost any other moment in her tenure because it said, "I trust you with the truth. And I believe we can navigate it together."

Elissar's story reminds us that communication isn't always about having good news. Sometimes it's about delivering hard news in a way that builds strength instead of fear.

Key Practices for Intentionally Resilient Communication

When it comes to communicating intentionally, you don't need fancy platforms or flawless delivery. Here are a few core practices I teach and use with my clients, especially when the stakes are high.

1. You can't overcommunicate during stressful or uncertain times.

People don't just hear your words. They feel your energy. When situations are uncertain, even silence becomes the loudest signal. If you're not saying anything, people will assume the worst.

Layer context into the message, then repeat the message. Reinforce the core idea through multiple formats, channels, and voices. Acknowledge the moment, even if you don't have all the answers yet. It's better to stay present than to disappear until the message is perfect.

2. Close the gaps.

Every organization has communication gaps between levels, functions, reality, and perception. During times of stress, those gaps grow. If you don't close those gaps, someone else will—with assumptions, rumors, or fear.

The fix isn't to add more messaging; it's to add more clarity. Ask yourself: *What information do people need to know right now to do their job? To make a decision? To feel seen and supported?*

Then share that information clearly, simply, and directly.

3. Create systems for shared learning.

One of the most overlooked forms of communication is knowledge transfer. When we solve something under pressure, we rarely stop to capture it. We're busy, so we move on to the next fire, and the learning evaporates so that no one remembers how the last person solved it. That's how organizations lose Intentional Resilience.

Intentionally Resilient teams write it down. They teach it forward. They create rhythms like standups, huddles, and Communities of Practice where lessons get shared, not hoarded. They honor institutional knowledge.

4. Choose *what* and *why*, not just *how*.

In every message, you have a choice. Are you pushing out updates, or are you shaping understanding? Are you trying to make people comply, or inviting them to contribute?

Communication that works is rooted in purpose. Know what you're trying to shift—an attitude, a belief, or a behavior—and name it. Then build your message to support that goal.

The Power of "I Don't Know"

Luca Fioravanti—the Group Head of Security for Dolce & Gabbana, whom you met in Chapter 5—has spent his career navigating high-stakes roles in global security and risk management. He's led teams through data breaches, geopolitical threats, and large-scale digital transformations. But one of the most powerful leadership moves he ever made was admitting what he didn't know.

Early in his transition to a new leadership role in Ireland, Luca was faced with unfamiliar cultural expectations and rapidly shifting technological landscapes. "There were moments when I simply had no answers," he recalls. Rather than bluffing or deflecting, Luca chose transparency. "I told my team, 'I don't know, but I'm committed to learning.' That sentence changed everything."

This simple declaration boosted his credibility. His willingness to admit uncertainty invited collaboration and created psychological safety. It gave his team permission to experiment, offer ideas, and learn alongside him. "That's how we built real innovation—through shared vulnerability," Luca said. "Sometimes, leading with humility is the strongest kind of leadership there is."

Leading with Levity

Aaron Tucker is a Senior Principal at Accenture and a former US Navy SEAL. Today, he leads teams through high-stakes decisions and complex engineering challenges. One of his most consistent tools is humor.

"It's not about being funny," he said. "It's about disarming the moment and giving people permission to show up as themselves."

Aaron uses humor to open conversations, especially when the stakes are high or the topic is emotionally loaded: a quick quip, a self-deprecating joke, or a comment that signals it's safe to be real.

"I've found that laughter creates an on-ramp," he said. "Once people laugh, they loosen. They listen differently. They speak more honestly."

For Aaron, humor isn't a detour from serious leadership; it's a bridge to deeper trust. And in a culture where candor fuels Intentional Resilience, trust is everything. Humor works in every ecosystem and with people of every age.

Summary

When situations are uncertain, pure information transfer—or worse, silence—is the default communication mode of Reactive Resilience. As we've seen, it can contribute to anxiety or fear as people tense up in response. But effective communication during challenging or uncertain times does far more than transmit information; it creates alignment, safety, and momentum.

Throughout this chapter, you've seen how Intentionally Resilient leaders use their voices to *connect*, not just to *inform*. They clarify the narrative in chaos and speak truth even when it's hard. They ask better questions and listen with real presence. And when needed, they give space for others to step in and contribute their voices.

Intentionally Resilient leaders communicate to empower, not to control. They understand that how you communicate during uncertainty becomes a blueprint for how others show up, respond, and lead in return.

Micro-Steps

This kind of communication creates a foundation of trust. And trust, more than anything else, is what allows Intentional Resilience to take root and grow.

Start here by reflecting:

- How do you practice "cognitive kindness"? What words or concepts could you strip out to make your message even clearer?
- What is your reflexive communications mode when you have difficult news? Why? How does it impact your energy and the energy of your team?
- How do you capture and communicate institutional knowledge?

Try these micro-steps:

These small practices will help you build Intentionally Resilient communication into the rhythm of your leadership:

- **Say it until it's boring.** If your message feels repetitive to you, it's just starting to land for your audience. Consistency builds clarity.
- **Close the loop.** Don't assume people know what's happening. Finish the story, even if the update is "Nothing has changed."
- **Context first, content second.** Frame your message by starting with why it matters, especially in fast-changing environments.
- **Create a listening space.** Build in time for feedback and reaction. Don't just broadcast, invite a response.
- **Use tone as a leadership tool.** The *way* you say something often matters more than *what* you say.

- **Model vulnerability.** Don't be afraid to say, "I don't know." It builds trust and shows humility in uncertainty.
- **Inject lightness.** A moment of humor or warmth can lower defenses and open dialogue.
- **Repeat your values.** In times of stress, remind people what you stand for and what stays true, even when circumstances change.

Effective communication isn't about mastering a script. It involves building habits that help others feel informed, included, and inspired, even in uncertainty.

When we communicate with intention, we lay the groundwork for collective and personal trust. It's what allows a group of individuals to become an Intentionally Resilient team—and part of a community, which is the next element on the flywheel.

CHAPTER 8

COMMUNITY— YOUR HIDDEN STRENGTH

"Resilience is a team sport," said Darin Wolter, the Chief Revenue Officer at Specright, and I agree. Even the most driven, competent, and visionary leader will buckle under enough pressure if they try to go it alone.

We love the stories of lone genius founders who "powered through," but those stories tend to leave out the part where the founders were surrounded by people who helped them get there, sometimes quietly and sometimes heroically. Yet, Intentional Resilience doesn't happen in isolation.

Marcus Grindstaff understands this at a molecular level. You met Marcus in the last chapter. He's a former CTO and COO who now serves as a board director for medical device companies, and he's also spent years coaching a high school robotics team. In a gymnasium, surrounded by teenagers and circuit boards, he's seen the clearest version of what a high-performing team looks like under pressure—and what it means to lead them *through* the storm without *being* the storm.

Marcus's team consistently ranks among the top five robotics teams globally. It's not just about talent or funding or the latest parts for the robots. It's about structure. The team runs with a two-tier leadership model: an executive team and a functional team, both entirely student-led.

They hold each other accountable, solve their own conflicts, and make high-stakes decisions together. They are not "led" in the traditional sense. They are empowered.

Still, Marcus guides them. His role is about infrastructure and intentionality, not hovering. He helps build the scaffolding so the team can operate in a crisis without him. When a major flood short-circuited their robot two days before a world-class competition, Marcus felt confident deferring to the students to solve the problem because they were already a cohesive team.

The traditional Reactive Resilience model makes us think that resilience is forged in hardship. But Marcus shows us that Intentional Resilience is forged by design, by letting go of the myth that we must be the strongest, smartest, or loudest person in the room. When we're surrounded by people who are prepared and empowered, we don't have to carry everything ourselves.

That kind of shared Intentional Resilience is what carries robotics teams to the finals, and leaders through the floods.

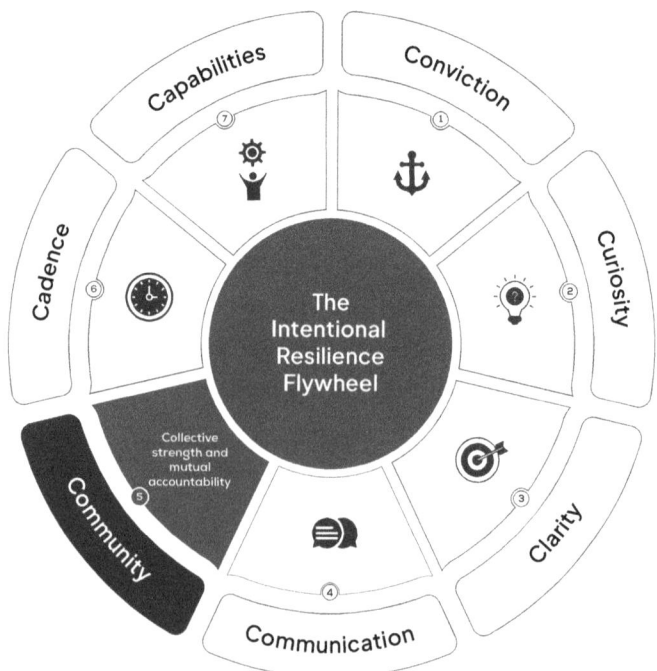

Real Community versus Performative Connection

Let's be real: the word "community" gets thrown around a lot in leadership circles. We say things like, "We're building community," when what we really mean is, "We have a Slack channel" or "We held an off-site." Those are not examples of true community; those are logistics.

Real community is a fabric that's woven over time with trust, consistency, and honest investment. It's the difference between optics and oxygen. One looks good in a quarterly update, and the other keeps you going when your energy's tapped and the pressure's high.

When I first moved to Austin to start my software company, I was starting over. New city, new chapter, and no roots. I didn't have a network yet. I had Google Maps and business cards. But I quickly met Bob Campbell. Bob is a longtime Austin legend, the kind of person who remembers your name, your last three jobs, your favorite restaurant order, and your biggest dreams.

Bob invited me to lunch, and it was warm and low-key, with no agenda. But here's the thing: At the end of that lunch, Bob offered to introduce me to two people he thought I should know. Then he asked me if I could introduce him to two people I thought *he* should know. And just like that, a rhythm began.

For several years, Bob and I met regularly for lunch. Each time, we both came prepared with the names of two people we could introduce to each other—other founders, investors, or just people we found interesting. It was never transactional. It was connective. We were weaving a web of trusted, respected connections for each other.

We didn't always know how those introductions would land, but they always added possibility, perspective, or support. Years later, that web became a lifeline.

Not long after I shut down my company, I was in a fog. The kind where you don't remember what day it is or how long you've been wearing the same outfit. I didn't want to talk to anyone. I definitely didn't want to show up for any event.

But a friend Bob had introduced me to invited me to her home. "Just come," she said. "No pressure. Just be there." I didn't want to go. But I went.

A few of us ended up on the porch late in the evening, tea in hand. Someone asked how I was doing, and I didn't have a polished answer. I cried. I didn't mean to, but I did. And no one looked away. They just made room, and that's what I needed in that moment.

That's real community. Not a curated moment, but a porous one. The kind where nothing must be fixed or solved or turned into an action item. The kind where presence is the offering, and trust is the currency.

Science backs this up. When we're with people we trust, oxytocin levels rise and cortisol levels drop. In other words, connection helps regulate our nervous systems. It's a biological strategy, not just an emotional nicety.

And yet, we keep treating community like it's optional or relegating it to "culture initiatives" and team trivia nights. But community isn't about programs. It's about permission and proximity: The permission to say, "I'm not okay today." The permission to ask for help. The permission to be human.

Proximity doesn't mean geography. It means intention. Do the people in your circle know what matters to you? Do you know what matters to them? Are you checking in when nothing's on fire, or only when something breaks?

Real community is built in the quiet moments—on the porch, at lunch, and in the "just checking in" text you sent without overthinking it or asking for anything back.

That's the difference: Performative connection is about visibility, but true connection is about community. One tries to look like a team, but the other functions like one.

So, how do we build this type of community so it's in place before we need it?

Building Your Community of Ecosystems

One myth we carry, especially as leaders, is that we need one person, or one team, who can "be there" for us in all the right ways. But remember that Intentional Resilience doesn't come from a singular source. It comes from an ecosystem.

That's why I talk about community in terms of ecosystems. There's the internal ecosystem made up of your peers, team, and work circle, and there's the external ecosystem made up of your mentors, former bosses, peer groups, and friends in other industries. More than anything, there's the cultivated mosaic of people who make you sharper, steadier, and more whole, in all areas of your life. The art is in the mix.

Al Reid, a healthcare veteran and board leader, lives this philosophy. Al led corporate strategy and mergers and acquisitions at companies like Abbott Labs, and now he serves on the board of Farmers Insurance. He has built a career defined by connection.

Al often tells young professionals to create a circle of trusted guides who reduce risk and create value in your life—people who challenge your thinking, reflect your values, and keep you honest. Al cultivated relationships more than he collected contacts, and he maintained those relationships as part of an intentional rhythm.

"You've got to stay in contact when you don't need anything," he said. "That's how you build trust."

That mindset paid off when Al's team needed to globalize a domestic business. They didn't have the in-house expertise to navigate the regulations, partnerships, and local leadership dynamics in Asia-Pacific markets, but Al did have the relationships. He tapped into his broader community of international operators, advisors, and cultural translators with the intention to build true partnerships. Trusted connections opened doors that would have otherwise stayed closed. People vouched for him, introduced him to local experts, and helped the company avoid common missteps. Because that ecosystem was built on mutual respect—not urgency—the help was real.

Your ecosystem doesn't have to be huge, but it does have to be honest. It needs to be tended, not just tapped. The people you surround yourself with help shape your perspective, your resilience, and your ability to recover from burnout or doubt.

Community includes those you've made space for over time, along with the information they can share. That's as true in life as it is in leadership.

Community as a Vessel for Knowledge

One of the most overlooked sources of burnout isn't overwork. It's hoarding.

The habitual kind of hoarding, where knowledge lives in one person's head and stays there because no one asks for it, or because it never felt like the right time to share. Or because the person who fixed the fire got pulled into the next one before they could explain what they did to put out the flames.

You've seen this type of institutional amnesia: One person knows the critical fix, solves it under pressure, and disappears before the knowledge is captured. The next time the same issue happens, no one else knows what to do.

If we want our teams to bend without breaking, we must intentionally democratize what we know: write it down, teach it, share it, and make it findable.

We first met Archana Arunkumar in Chapter 4. She's a product and technology executive who has built and scaled engineering cultures inside high-growth and Fortune 500 companies. But what she does exceptionally well is create a culture of psychological safety where knowledge moves freely.

Archana is intentional. She knows that when people feel unsure of their standing—politically, emotionally, or structurally—they don't share what they know. They protect it and silo it. That kind of withholding, even when unintentional, corrodes Intentional Resilience on teams.

So, Archana designs her teams with structures that invite sharing from the start. These structures show up in small but powerful ways—shared documents that capture updates and emotional context, spaces where engineers and operators collaborate, and a deliberate mix of introverts and extroverts in decision-making roles so information doesn't get stuck in one communication style. Most importantly, when things go wrong, she responds with calm curiosity—not punishment.

Archana also shared the story of implementing a "technology council" at a company mired in decision fatigue. By selecting respected individual contributors at all levels across the organization and tasking them with coauthoring the engineering priorities, she unlocked forward momentum. Buy-in became bottom-up, not top-down. Sharing knowledge and alignment on technical priorities was the way forward.

That's the difference the community element can make. In a culture of *fear*, people hoard information to protect themselves. In a culture of *trust*, they share it to protect each other. And it doesn't stop inside the organization.

Ciara Lakhani has been a Chief People Officer in multiple high-growth startups and is the founder of Elevate People. She shared how some of her most valuable knowledge exchanges happened outside formal channels entirely. Ciara is deeply connected to a peer group of other CPOs through WhatsApp, Slack, email, and phone calls. Her peers are her functional support systems, sharing hiring rubrics, onboarding templates, and even language for layoffs.

She said that the magic of those circles was in how fast and deep the help could go since trust was already present, and no one was trying to prove anything.

It reminded me that some of the most Intentionally Resilient knowledge ecosystems aren't formal at all. They're peer-based and trust-based—fast, quiet, and generous.

Celebrate to Sustain

If sharing knowledge keeps the *system* from breaking, celebrating wins keeps the *people* from breaking.

When you're running hard—especially in fast-moving, high-stakes environments—it's easy to move from project to project and fire to fire, without taking a breath. That's where burnout hides. Not just in overload, but in under-recognition.

Across the startup landscape, Ciara saw firsthand how organizations miss opportunities to reinforce accomplishments and foster connection. "If you don't celebrate it," she said, "it doesn't imprint." The work disappears into the noise, and people start to wonder if what they did even counted.

Al Reid made a similar point about how easy it is, especially for leaders of color, to get caught in the loop of proving and producing—without being seen. Celebration, for Al, wasn't just about acknowledgment but about legacy. About telling the truth, out loud and in the room, of what was built.

And then there's Oliver Albers, whom we first met in Chapter 4. He has spent years leading complex, cross-functional teams in high-pressure environments at Nasdaq. One of his earliest leadership lessons came during a startup acquisition. His team had worked brutal hours to deliver results in a fast-moving deal. The pressure was real, and the stress was visible. When the ink finally dried, Oliver paused the workflow and pulled the team into a room—not for a debrief but for a celebration.

Not everyone was comfortable at first. Some had never been publicly recognized before. But Oliver made it personal, thanking each of them specifically, not generically. Then he told a story from the early, messy days of the project, making everyone laugh. It wasn't just a celebration. It was a moment of cohesion.

Oliver said, "People remember how you made them feel more than what you delivered." That gathering became a touchstone. Months later, when another challenge hit, Oliver's team referred back to that celebration—not to the metrics but to the moment. It reminded them that they weren't just executing, they were *building something together*.

But connection isn't only about what happens at the finish line. It's what makes the work possible in the first place. And for that, we need tools. Not just policies or perks, but real practices that help teams feel seen, safe, and synced.

Team-Level Tools to Foster Community

Some of the most powerful tools to build Intentional Resilience aren't expensive or complicated. They're habits: small, repeatable signals that tell people "You matter here."

One of my favorites is the two-word check-in.

At the start of a meeting, especially when the stakes are high or the pace is fast, I'll invite everyone to share two words to describe how they're arriving—just two. No elaboration. Just a pulse check. You'd be amazed at how often those words change the room. "Intrigued + hopeful." "Frustrated + curious." "Quietly overwhelmed." Suddenly, we're not just performing, we're present.

And presence is the point. Tools don't replace trust—they scaffold it and help normalize care in fast-moving, high-expectation environments.

Other practices I've seen work well:

- **Peer story sessions**, where team members share the story of a time they overcame something difficult at work—not for show but to humanize the path behind the performance.
- **Gratitude rounds** at the end of sprints, where each person thanks someone else for a contribution, big or small.
- **Open office hours** that aren't for tasks but for unstructured check-ins and questions.

None of these activities takes a full day or a big budget. They simply create texture, context and space, building the kind of quiet trust that holds under pressure.

Build Communities Before You Need Them

The best time to build community is *before* a crisis. That may sound obvious, but you'd be surprised at how often leaders wait. They wait to check in until someone is visibly unraveling. They wait to share knowledge until someone leaves. They wait to build relationships until they need a favor. And by then, it's already too late.

Think of it like a savings account. You don't wait until the emergency occurs to start saving. You contribute over time so that when the unexpected hits, you're not empty-handed. Community works the same way. You show up when nothing's on fire. You check in when everything is quiet. You ask questions before someone burns out. You listen when the stakes are low so people trust you when the stakes are high.

That's how you build in peace for use in a crisis.

I've seen leaders survive unspeakable loss—of companies, loved ones, health, and identity—because they weren't carrying it alone. They had already created strong internal and external communities.

Santiago Aguilera, the Head of Corporate Affairs for Latin America at Mondelez International, lives on the front lines of volatility. He manages crises with government agencies, leads through misinformation attacks, and navigates shifting regulatory environments that can change overnight. When we spoke, he didn't start with a crisis. He started with trust.

"Create trust in peacetime," he said. "Not when the fire is already at your door."

This is why community matters. Not just for emotional support, but for insight. For data. For context that you can't get on your own. "Your network will help you adapt," he told me. "Sometimes to face a crisis, you don't need more opinions, you need better information. And you get that from people who see what you don't."

Santiago builds sustainable relationships rooted in reciprocity and readiness, nurtured before they are needed. When a crisis does come, he deploys those connections like an airbag—quietly, invisibly, and critically. That's the long game.

Summary

The communities we build in times of peace are the scaffolding that holds us up when all else feels like it's falling apart. No one can do the work of leading, working, and innovating on their own. That's why I include this line in my keynote: "Community may be one of our greatest competitive advantages."

Micro-Steps

Start here by reflecting:

- Do you schedule time to connect authentically with your community (inside or outside your organization or workplace)? If the thought of carving out time for these connections gives you heartburn, why?
- Is there a win you recently glossed over because you have too much else going on? Do you have a systematic way of capturing great moments, big or small, personal or professional?
- How do you capture and communicate institutional knowledge?

Try these micro-steps:

You don't need a full strategy deck to start building Intentional Resilience through community. You just need to start. Here are a few small, high-leverage steps to begin with:

1. **Reach Out When Nothing's Wrong**
    Send a short message to a colleague, mentor, or peer just to check in. No ask, no agenda, just presence. (If you know me personally, you have most likely been on the receiving end of one of these. A text to let you know I just met someone who looks like or sounds like you. A quirky photo of a meal that reminds me of one we shared together. It doesn't take much for me to feel inspired to reach out and connect for no reason other than to say, "You are on my mind! Hello!")

2. **Create Your Curated Circle**
    List five people who challenge you, support you, or bring clarity when you're stuck. Ask them how you can help them so you can continue to give back. These are your community anchors. Invest in those relationships regularly.

3. **Share a Win, Publicly or Privately**

   Acknowledge someone else's contribution this week. A Slack message, a voice memo, or a quick shout-out in a meeting or on social media makes the invisible visible.

4. **Start a Knowledge Thread**

   Choose one piece of institutional knowledge you're holding, and document it, such as a process, a lesson learned, or a template. Then share it where others can find it.

5. **Intentionally Create Cross-Functional Collaborations**

   Create a practice of pulling people together from unexpected areas. These collaborations foster curiosity, wider brainstorms, and innovation.

Start with one step and repeat it with intention. Every time you invest in community, you are investing in your future and building the foundation for Intentional Resilience. Now, let's turn our attention to cadence, the next turn of the flywheel.

CHAPTER 9

CADENCE—THE RHYTHM OF INTENTIONAL RESILIENCE

Cadence is the rhythm you lead by. It's not the schedule on your calendar or the speed your industry demands, but the deeper pattern beneath it all. The one that determines how you move through pressure, how you make decisions, and how you show up when the stakes are high and the answers aren't obvious.

It's important to distinguish cadence from speed and urgency. Speed is how fast you move; urgency is how fast you *feel* you need to move. But cadence is deeper: it's the practiced rhythm that lets you move at the *right* pace, not the fastest one. It's what keeps urgency from turning into panic. It's not just personal—teams, companies, and cultures all have cadences, too.

Without a shared rhythm, even the most talented people misfire, projects stall, communication frays, and the work becomes brittle under pressure. But when cadence is intentional—when there are clear signals, rituals, and expectations—the team doesn't just move, it moves *together*.

In my work with leaders navigating complexity, I've seen one pattern repeatedly: burnout can be caused by the volume of work and by the *velocity* of decision-making—with no space to think, breathe, or orient.

It's not the hard choices that wear people down. It's that we make them while sprinting from one task to the next.

That's where cadence comes in.

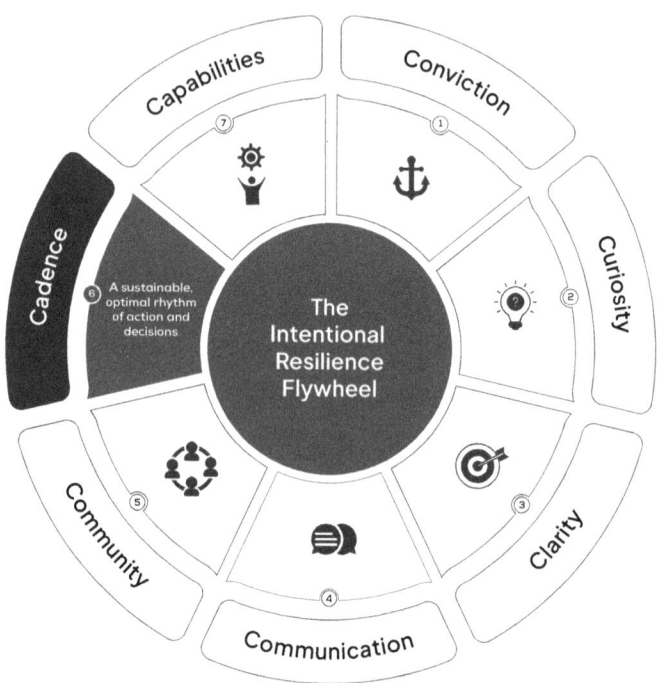

Intentionally Resilient leaders don't just act, they *respond*. They know when to slow down, when to speed up, and when immediate action is truly required. They understand the cost of reactivity, and they choose reflection when it matters most.

These leaders don't confuse stillness with inaction, or speed with strength. Instead, they build a bias toward intelligent action—action that's grounded, clear, and proportionate to the moment.

Cadence is what allows you to pause without paralysis, to move fast without panic, and to lead with presence instead of performance. And it's essential to the flywheel of Intentional Resilience.

Alongside conviction, curiosity, clarity, communication, community, and capabilities, cadence keeps the flywheel from spinning out of control.

It keeps momentum from becoming chaos. Without it, you can have all the right elements and still burn out. With it, each component has time to sync, strengthen, and support the others.

Cadence is the rhythm that makes Intentional Resilience sustainable. Let me show you what that looks like in motion.

The Captain Who Didn't Flinch

It was one of the most consequential decisions of his career—and he had less than forty-five minutes to make it.

Captain JJ Cummings—remember him from Chapter 7?—stood on the bridge of the USS *Gerald R. Ford*, the Navy's largest nuclear-powered aircraft carrier. After fifteen months in dry dock, she was finally ready to sail. The Secretary of the Navy had briefed the White House: she would launch at exactly 1:00 p.m.

Everyone aboard was new. No one on the bridge had ever taken this ship to sea.

Then, at 12:15 p.m., as they prepared to depart, someone approached JJ quietly: "Sir, we have a rudder issue."

In that moment, the stakes sharpened. If they launched and the rudder failed, they could run aground. If they delayed, they'd miss the tide window and break a promise to the White House. Most leaders would have reacted in a panic, but JJ did something harder: he paused.

He asked questions and stayed calm. When a two-star admiral walked onto the bridge, JJ met him with composure: "Sir, we're working through a minor issue."

Internally, he was burning. But externally, he gave his team room to think and to solve.

It turned out to be a faulty sensor. A misfiring dashboard alert, not a rudder failure. They launched twenty minutes late and avoided a crisis, damage, and a scandal.

That's cadence.

JJ calls it avoiding the "cobra strike"—the instinct to react before understanding the problem. In aviation, that reflex can be deadly. So, he trains his teams to pause, to breathe, and to literally count it out: *"One potato, two potato."*

That tiny delay can save the mission.

You might also remember Aaron Tucker, the Accenture consultant and former Navy SEAL from Chapter 7. He shared a principle from his combat training: *Get off the X.* In military terms, "the X" is the point of ambush, the kill zone. You can't freeze there. You must move off the X— quickly and intelligently.

For leaders, the X might be psychological, such as doubt, confusion, and panic. It takes skill to recognize when you're stuck and need to shift— not perfectly, but with purpose.

Intentional Resilience isn't always about holding your ground. Sometimes it means learning when and how to move.

The Discipline of Pacing

We spend a lot of time talking about how fast we can go. How quickly we can respond, adapt, scale, or ship a product. But speed without rhythm isn't Intentional Resilience—it's a risk.

Intentionally Resilient leaders know that the right speed isn't always top speed. It's the speed that matches the moment. Sometimes, that means *go now*. When the data's clear, the threat is real, or the window is closing, you move quickly and decisively. At other times, it means to *wait*. Sit long enough to gather yourself and think so you can see the full board.

The challenge with this approach is that we're not trained to vary our cadence. In high-performing environments, urgency can easily get conflated with importance. Everything feels critical. Every ping is a potential fire. And before you know it, you're reacting to reactions, caught in a cycle that exhausts you, burns you out, and erodes trust.

I've been there. I've let urgency drive decisions that needed deliberation, and I've also waited too long when clarity wasn't coming and a decision had to be made. Neither extreme builds Intentional Resilience.

What does? Pacing. The discipline to ask:

- Is this urgent or just loud?
- What's the risk of moving fast? What's the risk of waiting?
- What cadence does this moment require?

See, we either have a tendency to react viscerally and make knee-jerk decisions, or to wait for so long, paralyzed by indecision, that we metaphorically get "shot at" by waiting on the "X." Neither is a winning strategy.

Sometimes, the bravest thing you can do as a leader is to slow down. Sometimes, it's to speed up. But most often, it's to stay steady while everything else spins.

Cadence isn't just about *what you do*—it's about *when you move*. This is the difference between Reactive Resilience and Intentional Resilience. It means not being driven to react by the pressure of outside forces, but being intentional about the speed and direction in which you move when *you* decide to.

Cadence in the Real World

We've seen how leaders manage high-stakes decisions by deliberately controlling their pace. But cadence involves more than these pivotal moments. It's also about what happens between them, such as daily rhythms, cultural signals, and practices that anchor a team when times get noisy.

In the next section, we explore how consistency, intentional presence, and seasonal strategies help leaders build Intentional Resilience into their routines.

Fast, Not Frantic

Suzanne Dann knows what it means to lead when there's no time for hesitation. As the CEO of Wipro Americas, a global services organization, she continuously navigates complex transformations. She's made a habit of fast, yet precise, decisions. "It's not about rushing," she told me. "It's about being decisive in moments where clarity *can't* wait."

Suzanne recalled a moment in her career when a major client escalated an issue with global visibility. The details were messy, and the pressure was immense. Her team was looking at a multi-day analysis. But Suzanne assessed the situation and realized that the answer wasn't in more data. It was in the relationships. She picked up the phone and called the client directly. Within the hour, the tension broke, and the fix soon followed.

That kind of action requires two qualities: a bias toward motion and deep trust in your people. "You don't have to be perfect to be effective," she said. "You just have to move with integrity."

For Suzanne, cadence can be about slowing down to think *or* speeding up when the right move is now.

Every Season Has Its Own Strategy

Aaron Tucker introduced a valuable idea: cadence isn't static; it shifts with context. "Every season requires its own strategy," he said. His team moves in cycles, with intense sprints during product launches, followed by slower periods focused on systems and reflection.

Rather than aiming for constant balance, Aaron listens. He tunes the pace to match what's happening inside the business and within the team. "If you're in a growth sprint, call it that," he said. "Let people know it's going to be intense, but not forever." That simple act of naming the cadence gives boundaries to urgency and turns pressure into purpose. It also normalizes recovery. After every push, there's a pause—not as a luxury but as a strategy.

Cadence, for Aaron, is an active leadership skill and a way to honor the season you're in and help your team know they won't be sprinting forever.

Quiet Confidence Amid Noise

You last met Kim Nakamaru in Chapter 6, where she modeled courageous leadership through visibility and self-care. As General Counsel at fast-growth commercial rocket company Relativity Space, Kim leads enterprise-wide transformation initiatives and crisis response strategies. Here, she offers another lens on cadence: quiet confidence.

A colleague once told her, "Sometimes, you just have to sit your chair. Don't rush to fill the silence. Gather yourself. Then respond." That simple phrase—"sit your chair"—became a core teaching for her team.

In high-stakes moments—board meetings, disaster response calls, and leadership crises—Kim reminds her team to lead, not react. "When the room gets loud, sometimes the leader needs to get quiet," she said. "Not because they're unsure but because they're focused." For Kim, resilience lives in the pause and in the stillness before decisive action.

Structure as Stability

You first met Chris Hoffmann in Chapter 4. He leads a global privacy and compliance team at Robert Half. Chris describes cadence as the glue between chaos and clarity. "We have regular standups. Check-ins. Planning cycles. That rhythm lets us pivot faster when things change," he explains. For him, cadence isn't about routine for routine's sake. It's a way to keep the team aligned, even in turbulence.

His mantra is: "Be bold. Take intelligent risks. And if you fail, fail with reason." His teams know what to expect and when, which reduces decision fatigue and builds trust. Chris shows that cadence, thoughtfully applied, is a container that makes room for complexity without letting it spill into overwhelm.

Each of these leaders found their own rhythm by learning to listen to their teams, their environments, and themselves.

Cadence isn't a single tempo. It's the ability to tune your response to what the moment needs. And that takes discernment.

Let's talk about how to build it.

Evaluating for Cadence

It's one thing to believe in pacing, and it's another to know what pace the moment demands.

Intentionally Resilient leaders develop the judgment to shift gears and to sense when a situation needs urgent momentum or restraint. They learn how and when to "Get off the X." That kind of judgment can be built from moments of reflection, failure, and practice.

Over the years, I've started using a few internal questions when I feel the tempo of a moment trying to sweep me away:

- **Is this urgent, or just noisy?**
  Not every loud moment is a critical one. Some pressure is real, and some is just volume. Learning to tell the difference is key to developing Intentional Resilience.
- **Am I avoiding action or protecting clarity?**
  Sometimes, we wait because we're afraid. Other times, we wait because wisdom needs more space to surface. Delay doesn't always signal dysfunction. It can show discernment. Pausing can be powerful when it's intentional.
- **Is this situation asking for presence, movement, or a pause?**
  We often default to doing. But the most Intentionally Resilient move may be stillness—asking a question, or naming what's unclear instead of pretending we know.

I teach my clients these concepts, too: cadence is about pace and *fit*—the right tempo for the context and the right tempo for your body, brain, or team.

Cadence isn't just personal. It exists organizationally. Your company has a beat, and your team has one, too. When those rhythms get out of sync, situations fall apart, projects drag, misalignment grows, and fatigue creeps in.

Making Growth a Weekly Rhythm

Alain Luxembourg leads strategy and transformation across European markets for global cybersecurity company Barracuda Networks. He's known for pairing bold structural shifts with deeply human leadership. When his team faced a massive digital transformation, he didn't start with a roadmap. He started with rhythm.

Formal training wouldn't be enough because the change was too fast and the reality too complex. "People needed to grow while doing the work," he said. "Not in a workshop six weeks from now."

So, he introduced a simple concept: weekly learning loops.

Every Friday, the teams emailed a weekly message: one effort that failed, one thing they learned, and the top three priorities for the coming week. No slides and no hierarchy, just reflection and curiosity. This practice allowed the team members to reflect on their achievements and learnings of the week and build excitement for the week to come.

"It created this rhythm of growth," Alain told me. "People started showing up not just to report, but to teach. To admit what didn't work. And to get better—together."

Over time, the loops shifted the culture. Learning became expected, not an incidental side benefit. Feedback got faster, and fear got smaller.

The brilliance wasn't in the format; it was in the consistency. Cadence made it stick.

The most Intentionally Resilient teams have rituals to realign and check-ins that ask, "Are we moving at the right pace?" They have leaders who notice when someone's sprinting too long or not moving at all. And they include cultures that let people recalibrate without shame.

That's how cadence becomes Intentional Resilience for individuals *and* the entire organization.

Bringing It Back to the Flywheel

Cadence doesn't just *support* Intentional Resilience, it *powers* it.

Think of the full flywheel of Intentional Resilience: conviction, curiosity, clarity, communication, community, cadence, and capabilities. Each component has its own role, and cadence keeps them from colliding. It sets the tempo so that conviction doesn't become rigidity, clarity doesn't collapse under pressure, and capabilities don't burn out before they're needed.

Without cadence, you might be doing all the right things, but at the wrong pace. And that's what wears people down.

With the right cadence, you don't just endure complexity, you move through it with coherence.

In the next two chapters, we'll explore the leadership capabilities and personal capabilities that support this rhythm from the inside out. But first, let's practice, one beat at a time.

Summary

Pacing with intention isn't always about big decisions. More often, it lives in the small ones—the daily moments when you choose presence over reaction, clarity over speed. These are the choices that shape your rhythm.

Micro-Steps

Like any rhythm, cadence strengthens with practice. You don't need a life-altering event to start. You just need a few quiet steps in the right direction.

Start here by reflecting:

- When was the last time you felt the pull of urgency? Did the situation *truly* call for urgency? How might you change the cadence next time to optimize your response or decision?
- Think of a time when you found yourself "on the X." Which elements of the Intentional Resilience flywheel would have helped you navigate off it effectively and at the right pace?
- How do you discern between urgency and noise? What questions or filters do you use to distinguish between the two?

Try these micro-steps:

You don't need a crisis to practice Intentional Resilience. You just need a moment of awareness and a willingness to respond with intention instead of reflex.

Here are a few micro-steps to build your cadence muscle, one beat at a time:

1. **Name the Pace You're In**
    Each week, ask yourself: *Is this a sprint, a jog, or a recovery?* Then communicate the answer to your team. Let people calibrate expectations to match the rhythm.

2. **Use the Two-Beat Rule Before Responding**
    When urgency spikes, count: *one potato, two potato.* Then take action or communicate. Those two seconds often create just enough space for clarity.

3. **Mark the End of Your Workday**
    Create a simple ritual to separate your workday from the rest of your day. Turn off notifications, write a quick reflection, or shut down your laptop with intention. An Intentionally Resilient cadence includes recovery.

4. **Tag Your Emails**
    Add "Not Urgent" or "Can Wait Until Friday" in your subject line when possible. Normalize pacing cues inside your culture.

5. **Ask a Cadence Question in Your Next 1:1 or Team Meeting**
    Try: *Does our current pace feel sustainable to you? What would help right now—momentum or space?*

Start with one of the micro-steps above, and practice consistently. The goal isn't to move faster. It's to move with more wisdom, toward Intentional Resilience.

Let's pause here for an interlude about powering the flywheel.

POWERING THE INTENTIONAL RESILIENCE FLYWHEEL

By now, you've seen how you can design, not just hope for, Intentional Resilience.

You've explored conviction, curiosity, clarity, communication, community, and cadence. Each of those components builds on the others and adds stability, momentum, and lift. Together, they form a flywheel—a self-sustaining system that strengthens with every turn.

But a system, no matter how well-designed, won't move without energy. It needs power. It needs a push. It needs something that turns *intention* into *motion*.

That's where capabilities come in.

If Intentional Resilience is what carries you through complexity, then capabilities are the force behind it. They're the practical expression of every other component: the ability to act on conviction, pace decisions with clarity, foster psychological safety, communicate with care, and lead through uncertainty. Not just once, but repeatedly.

Capabilities are what give the flywheel torque.

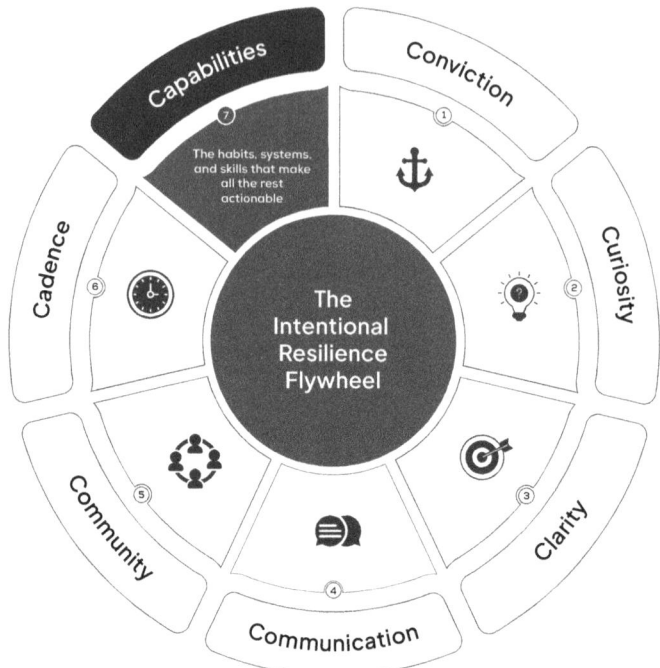

In the Intentional Resilience model, capabilities represent both strength *and* sustainability. They're how leaders stay grounded, flexible, and effective in the face of challenges. Because this element is so central, it deserves two chapters:

Chapter 10: Capabilities—The (Leadership) Power We Pass On looks outward at how you stretch your team, create conditions for growth, and lead through a crisis with trust and clarity.

Chapter 11: Capabilities—The (Personal) Power Within turns inward toward the daily practices that protect your energy, reinforce your values, and keep you human while leading.

Together, these chapters explore a truth I've seen repeatedly: Intentionally Resilient leaders don't rely on a single strength. They draw from a portfolio, a mix of emotional intelligence, strategic clarity, personal boundaries, and situational awareness. These skills are interdependent, dynamic, and deeply human.

Real leadership is always in motion. It lives in the way you shift gears under pressure, integrate feedback on the fly, and show up consistently, across roles, teams, seasons, and ecosystems.

These capabilities make you *more* of who you already are.

In the next two chapters, we'll cover capabilities, the final turn of the flywheel.

CHAPTER 10

CAPABILITIES—THE (LEADERSHIP) POWER WE PASS ON

You've taken leadership seminars, read the books, and put in the reps to sharpen your leadership capabilities. It seems as if you never finish learning how to lead people effectively. However, if you want to build an Intentionally Resilient team, one of your most important responsibilities is this: **You own the work of modeling Intentional Resilience for others.**

That doesn't mean adding another task to your plate; it means recognizing that you already model resilience *every day* through words and the way you build strong teams, shape the culture, and respond in the hard moments.

As Suzanne Dann, CEO of Wipro Americas, puts it: "Leaders must not only stretch and support their teams but also demonstrate resilience. How can you support your team if you're not feeling resilient yourself? Leaders must model resilience."

Your team is watching your strategy, and they are watching *you*: your energy, your reactions, and your recovery. It can feel daunting to realize your behavior is always being observed and dissected. It's also a powerful opportunity.

Brandi Joplin, the former CFO of Sam's Club, shared, "I realized my team was always watching for how I handled myself under grace and under fire, and how I encouraged or brought them along."

That's what leadership really is: modeling the kind of culture you want to create.

In this chapter, we'll explore five leadership capabilities that help you move from *doing* Intentional Resilience to *teaching* it—on purpose. Each one strengthens your team's capacity to build Intentional Resilience and reinforces the culture you're building. We'll explore how to:

1. Dissolve the Comfort Zone

2. Expand the Circle of Control

3. Normalize Failure on the Journey to Success

4. Decenter Yourself to Make Space

5. Take Ownership, Not Credit

However, before we go further, let's address a fundamental truth: **Leadership is hard.**

When people talk about leadership, they often focus on the individual: the charisma, decisiveness, or ability to hold a room. But some of the most powerful leadership capabilities don't begin with the leader at all; they begin with the team.

Strong teams are built deliberately, patiently, and often in moments when growth feels the least convenient.

I've coached plenty of brilliant executives who felt stuck because they were carrying too much alone. The issue wasn't *capacity* but *distribution*.

They hadn't yet built the kind of team that could move independently, think critically, or stretch into new challenges without fear. The team had the raw talent, but the leader hadn't yet invested in the people. They hadn't developed their team's resilience with the same intentionality they brought to their own.

The most Intentionally Resilient leaders I know are builders. They grow capabilities in others by hiring strategically, creating space for stretch, and adding a tolerance for risk. Most importantly, they give people clarity about what matters most, and they do it by design, not by default. Leadership isn't just about decisions or direction—it's about influence.

At the same time as you are building and empowering your teams, you are shaping the energy around those teams. People take their cues from you. When pressure spikes or ambiguity reigns, how you show up matters more than ever.

One leader told me, "I want to be authentic, but I also need to show gravitas." That tension is real. We're taught to be composed, even armored. But the best leaders have figured out how to be real without unraveling, calm without being cold, and decisive without shutting others down. It's a muscle, not a formula.

I've seen leaders manage their own heat by taking a walk before a tough meeting or venting to a trusted advisor like me so they can walk into a room with clarity instead of chaos. Offloading that tension with a trusted ear helps them release pressure and show up steady in high-stakes moments.

I've seen leaders normalize failure, like one who asked her team weekly: "What did we learn this week about what didn't work?" This question fosters growth, not shame.

I've seen leaders navigate layoffs with heartbreak and integrity, modeling compassion even when they couldn't control the outcome. And I've seen leaders take accountability quietly but completely by owning team missteps without pushing blame downhill.

Here's what all of that tells me: **Leadership is hard**. It's messy, multifaceted, and complex. It calls for emotional fluency, boundaries, judgment, and courage.

Here's the deeper truth: The resilience of your team starts with you, but it doesn't end there. To lead with Intentional Resilience, you must go beyond modeling. You have to teach it, build it, and shape it through systems, conversations, and culture.

That's where these five capabilities come in. They're practices, not theories. And they're how Intentionally Resilient leadership gets embedded, person by person, moment by moment. Let's take a deeper look at each of the five capabilities.

1. Dissolve the Comfort Zone

Intentional Resilience doesn't grow in easy terrain. It builds when people push themselves intentionally, just enough to realize they can.

"Getting out of your comfort zone builds resilience," said Doug Peterson, former CEO of S&P Global.

When work stays too familiar, teams lose the muscle that helps them pivot, handle ambiguity, or move under pressure. That's what happens when we stay safe for too long. What lives outside the comfort zone becomes ambiguous and uncomfortable—or downright scary—to navigate.

As a leader, your role is to build confidence in the unfamiliar—not to preserve comfort. That means teaching people how to "get off the X," move when stuck, stretch when it's tempting to stay still, and adapt when the landscape changes. And to do all this at the right cadence.

Lately, I've been obsessed with watching videos of NFL players doing Pilates or ballet. Athletes know the value of cross-training. They're building strength and agility. Leaders need to practice the same concept for their teams.

Ciara Lakhani, whom you first met in Chapter 8, is a Chief People Officer and the founder of Elevate People. When she found herself without a compensation lead on her team a few years ago, she could have taken the work on herself. But instead, she saw a chance to build capability into her team.

She approached a top-performing direct report—sharp, trusted, but untested in that area—and asked her to step in. The response? Uncertainty. "I can't do that. Why would you want me to do that?"

But Ciara didn't backpedal. She supported her, step by step, without taking the reins back. Today, that team member speaks on national panels, is quoted in Bloomberg, and is widely recognized as a compensation expert.

She was given room to become an expert. Ciara told me, "If I had done the work myself, it wouldn't have built capability into the team. Challenging her helped develop resilience for her individually, and for our whole team."

Stretch builds strength. When people realize they can get outside their comfort zones and recover quickly, they start to meet challenges differently. That's the quiet revolution of Intentionally Resilient leadership: showing your team that the edge of their comfort zone isn't the edge of their capability—it's the beginning of growth.

2. Expand the Circle of Control

Uncertainty is exhausting. When we don't know what's coming, our minds fill in the blanks with worst-case scenarios. The result? Worry, distraction, and a mental load that wrecks focus.

You can't remove all the uncertainty for your team, but you can change how people meet it.

One of my favorite tools for navigating uncertainty comes from Gwen Shaneyfelt, the Chief Administrative Officer for Franklin Templeton, whom you met in Chapter 6. When Gwen faces a challenge she can't solve right away, she puts it in a mental box. Not to ignore it, but to set it aside with intention.

"If you worry about everything every day, it just eats at you. I've trained myself—and others—to put things in a box. It doesn't mean you don't know it's there. It means you've made a choice: *not today*," said Gwen. Putting things in a box isn't avoidance. It's prioritization. It's how you protect clarity in high-stakes environments. Gwen's technique has become part of my own leadership language. I ask myself:

- What can I name, accept, and set down?
- What do I need to move forward with clarity?

- What belongs in the box—not because it's unimportant, but because it doesn't need to run the show today?

I teach the concept of expanding the circle of control regularly in workshops. I have leaders write down all the issues weighing on their teams, and then begin sorting: What's in our control? What's not? What can we influence? What needs to be put in a box for now?

The shift is almost immediate. At first, people feel powerless, but then the "in control" circle starts to grow. They realize more is within reach than they thought.

"People think they're completely out of control, and they become a stress ball. But when you write it down, you realize: *How I respond is a form of control,*" said Karen Stuckey, a former Senior Vice President at Walmart.

That effort represents the shift from fear to focus and from ambient threat to intentional action. Teaching people how to manage what's theirs to manage—and release what isn't—isn't just a mindset shift. It's a key leadership skill. When people feel in control, they move with more confidence and clarity. And without emotional drag.

3. Normalize Failure on the Journey to Success

Failure isn't defeat. This statement may sound obvious, but most teams don't seem to believe it. When failure is treated as a threat, whether explicitly or not, people start playing it safe. Curiosity shuts down, innovation stalls, and energy flattens.

That's why normalizing failure is one of the most powerful approaches you can take as a leader. Intentional Resilience isn't about avoiding failure; it's about learning how to move through it with speed, insight, and grace.

"Baseball is a perfect example. It's a sport where you could be in the Hall of Fame and fail seven times out of ten. Failure is part of the process. The key is learning not to be anxious about it and to learn from it," said Chris Hoffmann, Senior Vice President and Global Privacy Officer at Robert Half.

Normalization starts with psychological safety. Not as a buzzword, but as a real infrastructure. It means people feel safe to speak up, take risks, and admit their mistakes without fear of embarrassment or punishment.

That kind of safety must be built intentionally and operationalized in how you respond to loss, handle tension, and encourage your team to learn out loud.

"In SaaS sales, a 35 percent win rate is considered really good. That means you're losing 65 percent of the time. So, we ask: *What did you learn?* It's only a loss if you don't learn from it," said Darin Wolter, Chief Revenue Officer at Specright.

Your role isn't to protect your team from failure. It's to teach your team how to fail *smart* and move forward faster. That means:

- Help people learn to take intelligent, intentional risks.
- Model transparency when things go sideways.
- Shorten the learning loop with honest, blame-free debriefs.
- Encourage teams to experiment, reflect, and try again.

When failure becomes part of the rhythm—not an interruption of it—your team gets braver, more curious, and more adaptable. Failure isn't the opposite of success—it's how we reach success.

4. Decenter Yourself to Make Space

There's a leadership concept that's deeply counterintuitive, especially for us high-performing, do-it-yourself types. To build Intentional Resilience into your team, sometimes you need to step back. You need to ask, not tell. Not close the loop, but open it. This is the part of the flywheel where you model Intentional Resilience not by taking center stage, but by creating room for others to lead.

Early in my CEO career, a mentor gave me feedback that I'll never forget: "You shut down meetings too quickly." This was surprising to me. At the time, I thought I was being efficient by closing meetings and conversations quickly so I could give people their time back. But what my mentor helped me see was that some of the most powerful breakthroughs come after the agenda ends, in the space where other people are still thinking out loud.

So now, I purposefully leave more space at the ends of meetings.

Gwen Shaneyfelt, Chief Administrative Officer at Franklin Templeton, leads this way, too. She owns a massive operational scope, yet she still makes intentional space for others to speak and grow. She shared, "I believe in developing people in place. And sometimes that means stepping aside, not because I'm less invested but because it gives others the space to stretch."

One of Gwen's simplest practices is to begin meetings by asking her team to name their "big rocks," the real concerns or priorities that might otherwise get buried until it's too late to address them. She doesn't wait until the end of the meeting. Instead, Gwen begins with what matters most to her team.

It's a subtle shift, but it signals an important message:

- This room is for real conversations.
- This team has time for what's important to everyone.
- No one has to carry burdens alone.

I often apply this principle in coaching. I encourage leaders *not* to speak in every meeting, or even to lead every meeting. As a CEO, I've stayed silent in conference rooms just to observe. I've sent proxies in my place to empower others. It's remarkable what surfaces when you stop defaulting to the loudest voice in the room.

That's what this capability is about: not *doing more* but making *more possible for others.*

I built a tool called a "read.me" that transforms teams. The idea came from the dense manuals my engineers devoured whenever new hardware landed in our labs. In workshops, every team member writes their own. It's a user guide about themselves—how they communicate, what motivates them, and their values. When read.mes are out in the open, teams click faster with less friction and more understanding.

This isn't fluff. It's clarity. When teams share that depth of understanding, friction falls away and speed increases. People navigate tension faster, align more easily, and trust more quickly. Results land sooner, with less wasted effort.

This is what it means to decenter yourself:

- Step back to make room for others.
- Lead less and amplify more.
- Let your impact ripple through others.

Intentional Resilience grows when others learn they can lead, too.

5. Take Ownership, Not Credit

A mentor told me early in my CEO tenure, "Great leaders always fall on the sword for their team. But they don't take the credit when things go right."

I'll be honest. At the time, that advice sounded awful. I was a new CEO, working long hours, making tough calls, and carrying real risk. The idea of taking all the heat and none of the praise didn't sound noble. It sounded exhausting.

Over time, I learned that this is the essence of Intentionally Resilient leadership. When you model that kind of quiet accountability without blame or performance, you build something stronger than loyalty. You build *trust*. And trust holds the whole flywheel together. Without it, people won't lean in, stretch, or take risks. With trust, everything changes. Your team sees you own your missteps and lift others up in success. They stop bracing themselves, they believe you, and they follow.

"If you're in a situation where someone needs to take the heat, you can't blame your team. You step up. You defend the team. You build that trust. If a catastrophe happens, and you need to report it, you don't send the most junior person to speak to the press or regulators. You're the one to take responsibility. I always say: *Drop a ladder and bring people up with you*," said Elissar Farah Antonios, founder and CEO of Soul Ventures.

This capability means being *honest*, not perfect.

I'll confess that I've made missteps. As a CEO, I've misjudged vendors, picked the wrong offshore quality assurance team, and walked into a meeting with the CTO of a massive hardware company who turned out to be more competitor than partner. We were a resource-strapped startup, and it quickly became clear that the meeting was a one-way download of our proprietary information. (Whoa, that was an intense day of regret and hindsight!)

I owned these missteps instead of trying to bury them. I told my team about my mistakes, what I'd learned, and how we would adjust. And when they made mistakes? I protected them. No blame, just learning. And when we won? I pushed the spotlight toward my team every time.

Leadership isn't about looking good, it's about building something that *lasts*—a foundation of shared Intentional Resilience and earned trust. When you lead that way, your team feels safer and becomes stronger together.

The Power We Pass On

These five capabilities are daily, deliberate choices that shape how your team learns to operate, especially when situations get hard. They invite you to stretch your team instead of sheltering them. To help them focus when uncertainty clouds the way. To open the space for others to grow. To treat failure as part of the rhythm. To take ownership when things break, and to shine the light on others when they rise.

Intentional Resilience isn't a quality your team either has or doesn't have. It's an approach they absorb from how you lead. When you lead with intention—through systems, space, and trust—you don't just strengthen outcomes. You strengthen *people*. You build cultures that bend without breaking, and you pass on the capacity to recover, adapt, and move forward with clarity.

By empowering your team in these ways, you'll shift from Reactive Resilience to Intentional Resilience more quickly and smoothly. Remember, you are helping your team shift perspective. Nothing passively happens *to* them; by intentionally building these capabilities—expanding their comfort zone, normalizing failure, prioritizing innovation, and placing their wins at the center—you are ensuring that confidence, growth, and adaptability all happen *through* your team.

This shift is powerful. You are passing on the foundations of Intentional Resilience. That's the real work of leadership, and it's work we can all get better at, one micro-moment at a time.

CHAPTER 11

CAPABILITIES—THE (PERSONAL) POWER WITHIN

In the last chapter, we focused on how we show up for others. Now, we turn the lens inward. You can't build and support Intentionally Resilient teams unless you also build Intentional Resilience in yourself. Let's talk about how you show up for yourself. Life is hard, work is hard, and leading people while also caring for your family, managing uncertainty, and making high-stakes decisions that impact others can be exhausting.

Sometimes, you don't get to talk about what's weighing on you or the details no one else sees. It's easy to buckle under the weight of the responsibilities on your shoulders. In those moments, remember: If you want to show up for others with strength and clarity, you have to care for yourself with the same intention.

That's what this part of the Intentional Resilience flywheel is about. We'll talk about how you can stay anchored while you stay in motion. Just as you shape the energy of your team, you also shape your *own* energy. The choices you make to protect, fuel, and ground yourself give you the stamina to lead and live well over time.

In this chapter, we'll explore five personal capabilities that build and protect your energy:

1. Anchor Yourself

2. Protect Yourself

3. Fuel Yourself

4. Be Yourself

5. Surround Yourself

You can't lead with steadiness if you're constantly untethered or your foundation is shaky. That's why personal leadership starts with the quiet, deliberate capabilities that keep you grounded, even when the world around you feels unstable. These five capabilities are about leading from your center and learning to carry complexity without losing clarity.

1. Anchor Yourself

One of the most powerful choices you can make as a leader is to get crystal clear on what truly matters to you. This is about reflection in practice, not just in theory. It's about knowing your values, your priorities, and how they shape the way you make decisions whether the stakes are low or high.

The clearer you are, the more automatic your decisions become under pressure. It's like muscle memory. Once you've done the work of aligning, then you can just act.

When that clarity *isn't* there? Everything wobbles.

I've worked with leaders who drift from meeting to meeting, reacting rather than leading. They absorb the loudest energy in the room, they chase every urgent request, and then they wonder why their team seems confused or burned out. The same occurs in their personal lives. They chase, react, and burn out, impacting them and their families.

Without an anchor, you start leading from pressure instead of purpose.

- You say yes to projects that don't align with your values or goals.
- You pivot too fast—or not at all.
- And worst of all, you lose trust in your own judgment.

That's why anchoring matters. It's about *direction*, not just values. I often recommend that leaders write down their values on a sticky note, journal, or whiteboard so they are visible and grounding.

I've had a sticky note on my computer with my three core values for many years. It reads: Integrity. Respect. Transparency.

Those three values helped me make one of the hardest decisions of my career (and my life)—to shut down my company. They also carried me through everything that followed. Anchoring yourself in your values makes you unshakable and guides you in making wise choices in complex situations.

You can also anchor yourself in what's gone well and what you've already made it through. One of the most grounding and humorous stories I've heard came from Brandi Joplin, the former CFO of Sam's Club. After a meeting that didn't go well, she found herself spiraling into stress and doubt. A friend gave her a toy wand from the movie *Frozen* that played the song "Let It Go." Brandi kept that wand on her desk as a talisman for the next ten years. She didn't play the song often, but it was a visual reminder: *You can get through this. It's not so bad.* Sometimes, that's all you need.

Other leaders build rituals around reflection so they can stay grounded.

- Kim Nakamaru, General Counsel at Relativity Space, holds regular "board meetings" with her husband to check in on shared values and goals for their family.
- Darin Wolter, Chief Revenue Officer at Specright, blocks time each year to map a one- and three-year vision for his company and for himself. Then he ensures those visions align with his values.
- Alain Luxembourg, Regional Vice President, Western Europe, for Barracuda Networks, ends every evening by asking his sons three questions: *What did you enjoy today? What nice thing did someone do for you? What nice thing did you do for someone else?* It grounds them and helps teach his children to identify and appreciate their blessings.

These are grounding gestures, not grand ones. When you're clear on what anchors you, you'll spend less time reacting and more time leading from the center of who you are.

2. Protect Yourself

You already know life and leadership are demanding. What's equally important is knowing how to protect your energy so you can keep showing up at your best. That may mean setting boundaries, having a rhythm, and being unapologetic about what you need to thrive. Here's the truth: If you're not thriving, the people who depend on you—your team, your family, and your company—aren't either.

Burnout isn't a badge of honor. I had to unlearn that the hard way. Silicon Valley culture tends to treat exhaustion like a performance metric, such as how little sleep you had the night before, or how many all-nighters you've pulled this week. I stopped playing that game a long time ago. If I'm not showing up well-rested and on top of my game, I consider it a disservice to my clients, my stakeholders, and myself.

Protecting yourself doesn't mean checking out. It means being *intentional* about how you structure your days, your weeks, and your workload so you can stay grounded in the moments that matter most.

For me, that protection lives in micro-habits, small things I do repeatedly to foster my energy. For example, I try not to schedule calls before 10 a.m. unless it's critical. When I'm not traveling to deliver keynotes, I use my mornings to exercise, walk my dog, and prep meals so I can go into my long days feeling energized instead of depleted.

Unfortunately, I have had to learn (and re-learn) to protect my energy many times. I don't have it perfectly nailed down yet. After undergoing esophageal surgery a few years ago, my surgeon told me to avoid intense exercise for eight weeks. Then she instructed me to turn my energy dial down to 60 or 70 percent so I could rest and recover. This part of the conversation is burned into my memory:

I told her, "I don't have a dial. I have a switch. I go at 110 percent, or I'm switched off."

She said, "I've met your kind. You're going to have to find a dial. Because the switch won't work here."

Wipro Americas CEO Suzanne Dann limits her travel to a maximum of two cities per week. She said, "Any more than that, and it's a straight path to burnout."

Dr. Kim Abrego, COO of Disaster Recovery Services, whom you met in Chapter 6, takes it a step further. She opens her calendar to the whole company and includes visible blocks for rest, workouts, and thinking time. Doing so sends a signal that everyone has permission to schedule time for self-care and balance.

That's what protection looks like. It's not avoidance or control, it's purposeful self-leadership. This isn't about preservation, it's about modeling. When you show your team that rest and reflection are part of your Intentional Resilience leadership practice, you give them permission to do the same. When you set the rhythm of your days with intention, you don't just preserve your energy—you make room to grow it.

3. Fuel Yourself

Protecting your energy is critical. But protection alone isn't enough. You also have to know what fuels you and then give yourself permission to go do it.

I learned this the hard way as a startup CEO. I was working fourteen-hour days, seven days a week. The pace was relentless, the team was small, and everything felt urgent. There was always more to do and never enough time.

I was bordering on burnout until my best friend staged an intervention. She kidnapped me for a spa day. I resisted. She reminded me that the work would always be there, but if I didn't take care of myself, I wouldn't be.

That moment stuck with me. I've learned to spot the signs in myself when I'm running low: less focus, more irritation, and lower creativity. Now, I shift meetings, move deadlines, or pause entirely so I can recharge before I crash.

Ashley Black, the founder and CEO of Fascia Blaster, asks a million-dollar question: "How are you going to endure anything if you're not mentally and physically strong?"

Fueling yourself looks different for everyone. It might be physical, mental, emotional, or spiritual. What matters is that it's *yours*—and that you commit to it.

Sometimes, that means going surfing in the middle of a weekday. Darin Wolter, Chief Revenue Officer at Specright, tells a story about his first Executive Assistant. "She asked me what I loved to do. I said surfing, but I joked that I couldn't do it during business hours. She pushed back. She subscribed to an app that tracks the surf conditions, and would cancel meetings and tell me, 'You need to go surfing right now.' It felt irresponsible at first. But I came to see it differently: what's best for me is best for the organization I love."

And here's a cool little secret that Intentionally Resilient leaders know: You don't need entire weeks off to refuel. You can build micro-moments of energy right into your day.

Darin calls it "vacation math." Thirty minutes of rest or fun each day equals two and a half hours a week, ten hours a month, and 120 hours a year. That's three full weeks of renewal, without leaving town. Darin's micro-moments of fuel become a muscle that strengthens with time.

Fueling might look like journaling, music, meditation, exercise, birdwatching, tap dancing, or teaching balloon art at an assisted living home. (Yes, that last one's real. I've watched a longtime executive advisory client make the most remarkable balloon creations, and I've seen the stress melt off him as he does. It's quirky, fun, and remarkable.)

The point is this: You don't have to *earn* rest. You just have to recognize when you need it and trust that refueling yourself is an act of Intentionally Resilient leadership, too.

4. Be Yourself

My surgeon was right. I didn't slow down after my esophageal surgery. Instead, months earlier, I had scheduled a keynote for several weeks after the surgery, assuming I'd be fine by then. However, I was still dealing with unexpected complications that left me visiting the emergency room, unable to keep food down, and, thanks to air trapped by the implant in my esophagus, belching like a linebacker.

But I was committed to taking the stage for the closing keynote at a big sales kickoff. So, there I was standing in front of a crowd and holding a live microphone. I had no way to anticipate or control the air in the implant. So, I opened with: "I had surgery six weeks ago, and one of the complications is, well … spontaneous belching. I basically sound like a fraternity party right now. You've been warned."

Everyone laughed. I survived. But I learned something deeper that day—not just about authenticity, but about *vulnerability*. There was no hiding. I had to lead from where I was.

The word "authenticity" gets thrown around so often that it can start to lose meaning. But in the context of Intentional Resilience, it matters more than ever. If you're constantly hiding or shape-shifting by adjusting your voice, your presence, or your personality to match every room you enter, you'll exhaust yourself long before the work is done.

I once had a client who had just stepped into a new CEO role. She told me that she had different personas for each stakeholder group. When I asked her what happened when they were all in the same room, she paused. "I've never really thought about that."

It's not just executives. It happens to all of us. Kids recognize it, too. On a call with a client recently, I overheard her pre-teen pipe up from the other room, "Oh, that's Mom's *work* voice."

But the truth is, it's too draining to be anyone but you.

Everything you've learned so far in this book—about conviction, curiosity, clarity, communication, community, and cadence—only works if *you're the one doing it*. Not a version of you or a curated persona. Just you.

That's how Marcus Grindstaff leads. You met him in Chapter 7, as a repeat technology executive and leader of championship high school robotics teams. Across startups, enterprise strategy, and healthcare innovation, Marcus has built a reputation for steadiness because he doesn't try to be someone else. He brings the same intentionality to his time, his team, and his family.

"You don't need to have it all figured out," he told me. "You just need to be present. That's what people remember. Your presence, not your perfection."

That's what authenticity looks like in action. It means being real, rooted, consistent, calm, and human.

Archana Arunkumar, board director at Kwik Lok, put it simply: "By intentionally being more authentic, you grow your resilience muscle."

And here's the secret: When you stop performing, you don't lose credibility. You gain power.

5. Surround Yourself

Intentional Resilience is sustained, strengthened, and sometimes saved by the people around you. That's why this final personal capability is about consciously choosing who's in your corner and knowing you don't have to do this work in isolation.

We've already talked about how community is a competitive advantage in organizational life. It's also a personal advantage. Even the most grounded, values-driven leaders need people who can help carry the weight at times.

One of the most powerful ways to do this is by curating a personal board of directors: a mix of people from all parts of your life who can hold space, tell you the truth, and remind you of who you are.

This strategy doesn't need to be formal, and you don't have to send out agendas. You just have to know who you can call, whether you need a gut check, a reality check, or someone to tell you, "You've got this."

Brandi Joplin, the former CFO of Sam's Club, has a group like that. "My personal board of directors isn't just work people. My friend Shar-ilyn is my cheerleader. She always reminds me of what I'm capable of. And my friend Steve down the street tells it to me straight, even when I don't want to hear it. You need all flavors. Different people help you through different things."

Surrounding yourself with a support team involves taking the time to refill your cup with people in all your ecosystems, putting down your phone, putting on an out-of-office message, and reconnecting with others at a deeply human level. I'm always struck by how energized and human I feel when I unplug and reconnect with the people I care about—the ones it's easy to lose touch with amid the chaos of running a company and constant travel. They are a lifeline.

Remember, the point is about support. It's letting yourself be seen and held and offering the same in return. While leadership may feel lonely at times, it was never meant to be a solo endeavor.

Leading Through Extraordinary Events

Karen Stuckey knows how to lead under pressure. You first met Karen in Chapter 5. As a former Senior Vice President at Walmart, she managed a multibillion-dollar portfolio, making decisions that moved entire markets. Her days were packed, and her team relied on her. And then, her world shifted.

Her mother-in-law was diagnosed with dementia and could no longer live alone. Karen and her husband became full-time caregivers. No one else in the family could do it.

So, they built an accessible suite in their home. Every morning, Karen began her day on her knees, helping her mother-in-law shower in a roll-in bathroom, and coaxing her through resistance and sometimes through tears. Then Karen would dry off, change clothes, and step into a high-stakes leadership role.

"It's hard to be a leader with so much else going on in your brain," she told me. "There were days I'd sit in the garage and cry before I walked into the house."

And yet, Karen showed up at the office and at home. Not perfectly. Not performatively. But fully.

Karen didn't try to compartmentalize the situation or pretend it wasn't hard. She held both realities with grace: the emotional labor of caregiving and the strategic demands of her role. One didn't cancel the other. Both mattered.

Her strength came from her values: empathy, loyalty, and presence. It also came from the quiet capabilities we've explored in this chapter: the ability to stay grounded, to ask for help, to protect energy, and to keep leading through the storm.

So many leaders are carrying more than one reality, including public expectations, private pains, big jobs, and quiet battles. In those circumstances, Intentional Resilience is about staying present without losing who you are.

The personal capabilities we've explored here don't shout, and they don't need to. Their strength rests in steadiness and in the daily choices to reset, reframe, and remain engaged when it would be easier to check out.

That's what Intentional Resilience is: the practiced ability to stay human in hard moments, and to lead yourself first so you can lead others well. These leadership capabilities enable you to lead through disruption, uncertainty, and change with clarity and creativity.

Even if you belch onstage sometimes!

CHAPTER 12

INNOVATING YOUR WAY OUT OF CRISIS

We began this book by contrasting *Reactive Resilience* with *Intentional Resilience*—showing you how building the muscle of preparedness helps fuel an incredible competitive advantage in your leadership and your life. You may remember Pelton Shepherd from Chapter 2, the fifty-year-old, family-owned company that intentionally innovated ice packs that can be turned into plant food, are drain-safe, and are completely biodegradable. Pelton Shepherd isn't responding to negative external pressures or a crisis to innovate. Instead, the company is proactively getting ahead of the market, delighting customers, and seeing opportunities long before its competitors do.

But sometimes, a true crisis *does* happen. That's why this chapter is near the end. You've already learned how to build a proactive approach to Intentional Resilience. You've internalized the components of the flywheel. You've seen how Intentional Resilience gives you a competitive edge—and now, you'll learn how it prepares you for when things truly *do* go awry.

Crisis has a way of revealing our identity as leaders. It tests more than our strategy. It tests our reflexes, mindset, ability to create clarity in chaos, and, most of all, willingness to evolve.

As you know, Intentional Resilience isn't just about bouncing back. It's about building forward. Similarly, in the most disruptive moments, innovation can move beyond a mere survival skill and become a competitive edge in parallel.

Our world is unpredictable. Markets shift, expectations rise, and complexity compounds. You can't rely on a playbook. You need something deeper: a practiced ability to adapt in motion.

That's where Intentional Resilience and innovation intersect, especially in times of crisis. In those moments, innovation isn't a luxury; it's a leadership imperative. Intentionally Resilient leaders don't just recover. They reimagine. They act with clarity in complexity. And they do it by preparing in the quiet seasons.

That's how Santiago Aguilera leads. You met Santiago in Chapter 8. As Head of Corporate Affairs for Latin America at Mondelez International, Santiago's scope includes regulatory strategy and environmental, social, and governance, as well as brand protection and employee engagement across a region known for volatility and rapid change. His leadership is built on a core belief: You can't wait for a crisis to build your response. You prepare for it, intentionally and early.

Santiago is not a crisis *manager*. He's a crisis *strategist*. When Mexico proposed a potential tariff increase that could have upended his company's operations, his team was ready. They had already modeled worst-case scenarios, mapped regulatory pressure points, and nurtured government relationships long before the headlines hit. They didn't react—instead they were intentional and proactive.

That balance shows up in how Santiago trains his team to operate: sharp scenario-planning, fast internal alignment, and constant learning. After every disruption, they debrief on what happened and how they responded. Intentional Resilience, for Santiago, isn't innate; it's built.

"It's a muscle," he said. "You have to train it. And the only constant is change, so you prepare by practicing."

That mindset helped Santiago lead through one of the most challenging moments of his career: managing a brand under attack from fake news.

Misinformation was spreading fast, triggering concern among consumers and confusion among employees.

"There are two learning modes," Santiago told me. "Peacetime and crisis. Learning from a crisis is far more intense. We need urgency during a crisis, but not paranoia. It's a balance, moving fast without falling into fear."

Santiago didn't wait to contain the situation. He rapidly activated his network, stabilized internal communication, and brought key messages to market. His rapid response worked. Not only did the company navigate the attack, but it also came out stronger, its reputation enhanced by the clarity and speed of its response.

What made the difference? The relationships Santiago had invested in before the crisis.

"You don't build trust in the middle of the storm," Santiago said. "You build it in peacetime—so it's there when you need it."

This is Santiago's innovation muscle:

- Prepare early.
- Train consistently.
- Act fast.
- Learn everything.

Santiago takes the company beyond the mindset of "How do we simply react to what's happening *to* us?" and asks, "How can we learn and grow in parallel *through* this?" He doesn't view a crisis as an exception to innovation and growth but sees it as part of the business cycle.

Innovate While You Stabilize: Running Parallel Tracks

Crisis has two demands at once: immediate action and long-term vision. Crisis leadership often means running those tracks in parallel—managing volatility in the short term while building what's next in the background.

This dual lens—stabilize and experiment—requires both perspective and control. Too much pressure, and people freeze. Too little urgency, and they coast. The most effective leaders create a climate where risk is encouraged but never reckless.

You first met Luca Fioravanti in Chapter 5. He is the Group Head of Security for Dolce & Gabbana. He has led global teams through security, business continuity, and operational transformation in some of the most tightly regulated sectors in the world. In one case, a telecom partner experienced a massive service outage that disrupted connectivity across multiple enterprise clients. The fallout could have been severe, including damaged trust, lost business, and a long recovery curve.

But Luca's then-CEO saw the moment differently. "He said, 'Let's use this situation. Let's go above and beyond to support our clients now. Then, when this is over, they'll remember who showed up.'"

Rather than minimize the situation or delay action, the company mobilized instantly. Luca's team deployed a dedicated recovery squad, created temporary workarounds, and offered real-time visibility to their customers throughout the incident.

What began as a disruption turned into an inflection point. The clients stayed and deepened their partnerships. Within six months, that same line of business expanded because the company had demonstrated reliability and Intentional Resilience in action.

"Resilience isn't just about surviving," Luca told me. "It's how you transform difficulty into opportunity for your customers, for your employees, and for your future."

Intentional transformation is what carried Vinod Sood through one of the most volatile periods in his industry. As cofounder and Managing Director of Hughes Systique, Vinod watched his telecom client base shrink rapidly during sector-wide consolidation. Instead of retreating, he built forward by launching a dedicated innovation team to reposition the company across new verticals, from retail to healthcare.

Vinod's team was parallel pathing by managing operations while reimagining the company's future. "We don't wait for recovery," Vinod told me. "We prepare for it by building the future in parallel."

I've coached many leaders like Vinod. They don't wait for conditions to stabilize before they innovate. They build in motion. They reinvest when others are cutting back. They stretch their teams—not because it's safe but because they've done the groundwork to stretch wisely.

What strikes me about Vinod's story is the rhythm. His team at Hughes Systique used industry contraction as an opportunity to invest in capability. They made it a habit to reposition themselves. During the telecom collapse, they shifted to adjacent verticals. During the pandemic, they poured time into cross-training and readiness. During the economic slowdown in 2023, they had teams build AI prototypes. And now, in the AI surge, they're not scrambling. They're ahead of the curve.

That's the move. You don't need ideal conditions to grow. Instead, you need the judgment to know what kind of growth your circumstances allow. A crisis reshuffles the deck of what's possible. If you've done the internal work, if your team trusts each other, and if your systems are elastic, then disruption becomes fuel for positive movement forward.

Those who wait for certainty miss out, and those who continue building while others freeze? They win the game.

Peacetime Preparation

The Intentionally Resilient leaders who innovate their way out of crisis rarely start building their strategy the moment the disruption hits. They begin long before. By the time you're in the thick of it—scrambling for alignment, searching for support, and trying to restore trust—it's already too late to lay the foundation.

That's why resilience starts in peacetime. For Dr. Kim Abrego, COO of Disaster Recovery Services, crisis isn't an outlier. It's part of normal operations. Her approach is to design relationships that can hold under pressure.

"You don't want to be forming relationships post-event," Kim told me. "That's too late. You need trust in place before you need it."

That trust is built on shared values, aligned expectations, and consistent communication long before situations go sideways.

When you've invested in the infrastructure of trust, you move faster. You absorb disruption with less friction, and you recover with more clarity.

This kind of preparation is a deliberate choice. It shows up in the habits you build with your team, the scenarios you walk through in off-hours, and the routines you rehearse because you expect to respond well when a crisis arrives.

This is where a few of the earlier components of the Intentional Resilience flywheel come alive:

- *Conviction* keeps you aligned under pressure.
- *Clarity* helps you focus the team.
- *Community* ensures no one is carrying the weight alone.
- *Cadence* allows for strategic pauses and re-acceleration.

Preparation is about capacity, not prediction. It's about building the mental, emotional, and operational strength you need to stay upright when life bends.

It's the leadership version of muscle memory built by:

- Scenario simulations.
- Pre-defined crisis roles.
- Pre-cleared communication channels.
- Check-ins with stakeholders during calm periods, not just chaos.
- Parallel teams, one managing the crisis and one strategizing and converting it into future opportunities.

When the moment comes, you won't have time to think about what kind of leader you want to be. You'll lead from who you already are.

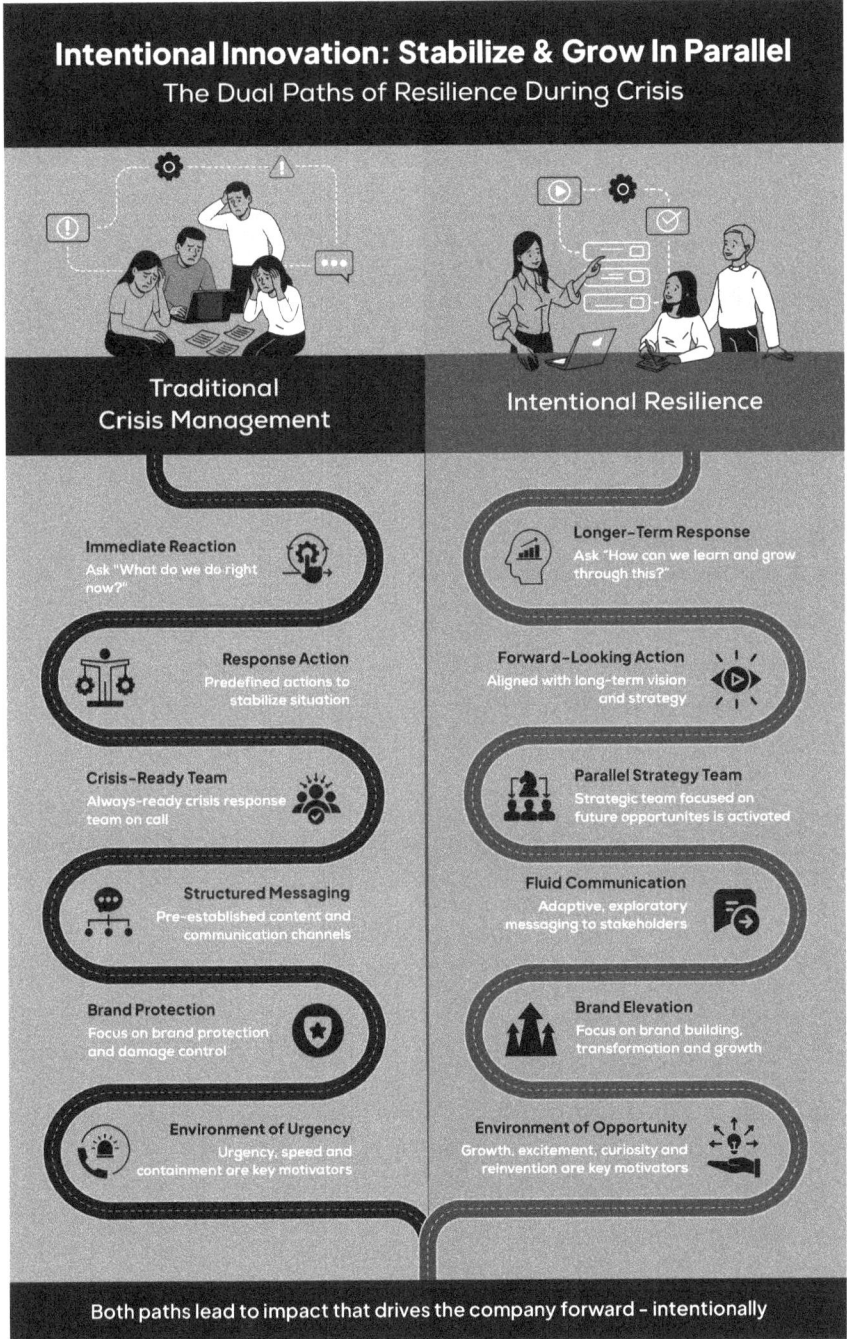

Focus Fuels Innovation

Crisis compresses everything—timelines, attention spans, and tolerance for ambiguity. It also creates the powerful element of focus.

The Intentionally Resilient leaders who innovate through disruption don't chase everything at once. They tighten the lens and prioritize what matters. They use the constraints of the moment to fuel clarity, not chaos.

Santiago Aguilera calls this skill the power of narrowing the aperture: "In crisis, our focus sharpens. We can't do everything, so we learn to focus on what we can influence."

That type of clarity doesn't appear on demand but is built in advance. Chris Hoffmann, Senior Vice President and Global Privacy Officer at Robert Half, emphasizes that focus under pressure is about structured readiness, not heroic improvisation. "You need your roles clear, your questions ready, and your decision-making frameworks practiced. Because in crisis, your brain doesn't default to brilliance. It defaults to routine."

That tendency to default is the real risk. If your leadership habits aren't intentional, pressure will expose them or, worse, define them for you.

The most Intentionally Resilient teams don't wing it. They prepare for focus, design for agility, and treat constraint as a creative filter, not a barrier.

This is how a crisis becomes an accelerant for innovation. Not because it's easy. But because the pressure doesn't leave any room for the actions that don't matter.

When It's Not a Crisis—Yet

It's easy to focus on leadership in the heat of the moment when the stakes are visible, the pressure is high, and the consequences are immediate.

But the most Intentionally Resilient leaders don't wait for the crisis. They build capacity before they need it. They develop the systems, the relationships, and the self-awareness that hold steady when disruption comes. They don't expect failure; they expect reality. And reality moves fast.

Chris calls this preparing under calm conditions. "You can't simulate the pressure of a real crisis, but you can build the infrastructure. You can walk through the steps. You can reduce the unknowns."

Preparation is both logistical and cultural. It shows up in how you invite curiosity, normalize learning, and reward risk—during stable times *and* during high pressure moments.

Stability is temporary. But readiness? That's something you can build.

I've seen it repeatedly in my coaching work. When leaders have taken the time to define their non-negotiables—how they lead, what they protect, and how they make decisions under pressure—they don't scramble when the moment hits. They act and create structure inside uncertainty.

"You don't have to solve this today," I often tell my clients. "But give yourself forty-eight hours to take the first step. Give the team one week to realign. Give the decision a check-in date, even if you're not ready to make it yet."

You don't have to pretend the entire situation is clear, but you can still lead with clarity.

Set a Deadline

I once coached a senior executive who was working in a deeply toxic culture. Her workload was unsustainable, her boundaries were ignored, and she was slowly burning out because she was being asked to compromise everything she stood for.

However, she didn't feel like she could leave the organization. She felt loyalty alongside fear. She had a dozen reasons to stay. So, I asked her to do something simple: set a personal deadline.

"If the culture doesn't change by this date," I said, "you'll know it's time to go. Not because you failed but because you gave the system a chance, and it didn't meet you."

She set the date, and she kept showing up at work with clarity and integrity. But the culture didn't shift, and so she left. What happened next was extraordinary. Her entire team followed her to her next role. She didn't ask them to, but they chose to because they saw what it looked like to lead with alignment. She walked away and toward a better option, on her terms.

That's preparation, too. It's knowing when to hold the line and when to let go. It's building the muscle to *choose* how you move forward. Your work is not to predict when a crisis may arrive but to prepare for who you'll be in the midst of it.

That's why, when I work with leaders on innovation, I don't start with strategy decks or brainstorming sessions. I start with how they…

- Move through complexity.
- Respond when the old playbook breaks.
- Carry themselves when the room gets quiet and everyone's waiting for a cue.

Innovation is a capability, a way of thinking, and a practiced fluency under pressure. And that fluency is forged in advance.

Build It Before You Need It

Crisis doesn't wait for permission, and it doesn't care if you feel ready.

Intentionally Resilient leaders rehearse rather than react. They invest in trust and build the systems, skills, and insights that will carry them through uncertainty, long before the pressure hits. In moments of rupture, you need to be able to lead from who you already are.

When you've trained for clarity, collaboration, and calm, creative motion, those same muscles will carry you through anything.

This is the real power of Intentional Resilience: You learn to withstand *and* to reframe. To recover *and* to reinvent. The leaders who innovate their way out of crisis don't wait for conditions to improve. They move, they focus, and they act.

In doing so, they don't just recover faster. They gain ground while others stall. They expand while others retreat. They create options while others cling to what's familiar. It's intentional, practiced, and real leadership—not luck.

In moments of disruption, your ability to move forward calmly, clearly, and creatively is your competitive edge, and it can make all the difference.

CHAPTER 13

ACTIVATING INTENTIONAL RESILIENCE

My hope is that by now, you see—and believe in—the benefits of Intentional Resilience. If you do, it's time to get tactical. I'm frequently asked, "How can I take this to my team, share this with my organization, and bring this into my life?" It's why I facilitate so many corporate workshops and senior leadership retreats where we focus on embedding Intentional Resilience into the DNA of teams and organizations.

I shared the leadership and personal capabilities of Intentional Resilience in Chapters 10 and 11, and now it's time to look at it from a systems level. We'll cover how to scale Intentional Resilience, nurture and activate it, hire for it, embed it into everyday work, and measure it to show the ROI.

Intentional Resilience has to live beyond individual moments—in the culture and in how you hire, onboard, run meetings, debrief after failure, recognize growth, and reset after hard stretches.

If you want Intentional Resilience to scale, you must design for it—intentionally, operationally, and every day.

Let's talk about how.

Embedding Intentional Resilience Into Everyday Work

For Intentional Resilience to endure, it must show up in how we work, every day, in every system.

That means designing Intentional Resilience into the mechanics of your team. It's a throughline, not a side note. Here's how:

1. **Hire for Intentional Resilience**

    Start at the door. Look for people who know how to navigate ambiguity, take feedback as a tool, and are curious about what they don't yet know. Ask how they've responded to failure or unexpected pivots. Ask what's changed in them after their last hard season? If they can't reflect, they're not ready to lead.

2. **Set Clear Expectations**

    Intentional Resilience starts on day one. Set the tone with clear expectations around learning curves, psychological safety, and communication. Let people see that failure isn't punished, and learning from it is rewarded. That's how you unlock curiosity and accelerate trust.

3. **Build Feedback Loops Into the Rhythm**

    Make space for Intentional Resilience to evolve. Host quick debriefs after projects, even small ones. Ask: "What stretched you?" "What helped you recover?" "Where did we move with clarity, and where did we miss the mark?" Make Intentional Resilience part of your team's self-awareness.

4. **Measure What Matters**

    If it's not visible, it won't scale. So, measure what you model. Track growth in flywheel areas: Is communication improving? Are teams managing cadence more intentionally? Are failure conversations becoming normalized? You can even use digital cues— like sentiment tracking in Slack channels or team surveys—to spot signs of waning psychological safety, tone shifts, and cultural friction points before they turn into issues.

This is where I think of the words that Vinod Sood, the cofounder and Managing Director of Hughes Systique, once told me. When I asked how he kept his team focused during industry volatility, he said, "When people feel purpose, they stay positive. They grow. They stop fixating on the short term."

Embedding Intentional Resilience is a long game. The secret is to make sure people know that what they're doing matters, today and in the long run, beyond the paycheck, the headlines, and the sprint.

When you create a culture of meaning and mutual care, people don't just *endure* challenges. They lean into them and see the *opportunities* on the flip side of each one.

Hiring for Intentional Resilience

If you want to build a culture of Intentional Resilience, it starts with who you hire. Here are a few interview questions that signal an openness to developing a "through you," not "to you," mentality.

1. **"What are you learning outside your area of responsibility right now, and why?"**
    Signals: Reflection, self-awareness, flexibility, emotional maturity, curiosity

2. **"When have you stretched outside your comfort zone, and how did you get comfortable with it?"**
    Signals: Growth mindset, coachability, flexibility, adaptability

3. **"How do you distinguish between noise and true urgency?"**
    Signals: Conviction, focus, clarity, situational awareness, emotional intelligence

4. **"How do you tend to react when plans fall apart or go awry?"**
    Signals: Flexibility, self-awareness, clarity, emotional intelligence

5. **"What's something hard you're proud of—not because it went well but because of how you handled it?"**
Signals: Aligned persistence, integrity under pressure, conviction, clarity

6. **"When do you ask for help, and when do you hold the line?"**
Signals: Judgment, boundary-setting, collaboration style

7. **"How do you reset after a tough day or week?"**
Signals: Self-awareness, emotional regulation, balance, adaptability

Use these questions to listen for how a candidate navigates complexity, relates to others, and reflects on their own growth. That's where real Intentional Resilience lives.

Measuring What Matters

For Intentional Resilience to stick, you must make it visible. One question I often get from executive teams is: *Can you measure something like Intentional Resilience?*

The answer is yes, if you're looking at the right signals.

It's possible to create KPIs around the results of building a more Intentionally Resilient organization. You can measure:

- How long does it take your team to move from a problem to a resolution?
- How often are issues buried versus surfaced early?
- Are tough conversations happening, and are they productive?
- How willing are people to ask for help?

Alain Luxembourg, the Regional Vice President, Western Europe, for Barracuda Networks, said, "If someone struggles for more than ten minutes, they should ask for help, and we should measure how often that happens. Because asking for help is a resilient behavior."

You can also use affect and tone as indicators. Ciara Lakhani, Chief People Officer and founder of Elevate People, suggests tracking emotional swings—not to police mood but to spot early signs of burnout. "If someone's energy and attitude are swinging too far, that's a signal," she told me. "Resilient teams don't have to fake being fine, but they shouldn't be whiplashing, either."

Archana Arunkumar, Board Director at Kwik Lok, offers another lens on measurement. Leading large technical teams through high-pressure transformations, she tracks signals of resilience by combining culture-building practices with operational data. "I believe in giving people enough context and then stepping back," she told me, "but I also want to see metrics that validate the work is being done well and can be repeatable."

While outcomes are what truly matter from a business sense, she also monitors the rhythm of engagement that leads to that output—things like continuous integration or continuous delivery cadence, defect resolution trends, and the time it took to complete root-cause analyses. Those markers help her spot burnout, confusion, or resistance before they show up in missed milestones. Intentional Resilience, in her view, is as much about information flow and trust as it is about sustainable performance—and you can measure all three.

In performance reviews, you can assess indicators like:

- How clear are you on our organizational goals?
- What tough moments did you work through with clarity or community?
- How did you pace yourself during intense cycles?
- What actions have you taken to strengthen your capacity to innovate or solve challenges?

Micro-Practices for Teams and Leaders

Intentional Resilience isn't just built in the big moments. It's built in the micro-decisions you make day by day, conversation by conversation.

Here are a few ways to build those muscles intentionally:

1. **Daily Reset**
   At the end of each day, or even between meetings, ask:
   - What's mine to carry?
   - What can I release?
   - How do I want to show up next?

2. **Recovery Check-ins**
   Start your weekly team meeting by asking, "Where are we challenged, and where do we need recovery?"

3. **Storytelling for Strength**
   Once a month, invite someone to share a "failed attempt" that led to growth. Make it normal and safe.

4. **Flywheel-Based Feedback**
   Anchor praise and feedback in flywheel terms. For example:
   - You're showing more conviction in your decision-making.
   - You brought curiosity into that client conversation.

5. **Growth Debriefs**
   Ask post-project:
   - Where did we stretch?
   - What shifted?
   - How did we recover?

6. **Personal Flywheel Reflections**
   Once a quarter, consider these questions:
   - In which flywheel capacity have I grown the most?
   - What area should I strengthen next?

These micro-practices will enable you to keep Intentional Resilience top of mind and help you consistently reinforce it with your team.

The Prickly Pear Council

Intentional Resilience isn't always loud; sometimes, it shows up quietly— through faster decisions, tensions named earlier, and a team that stays steady under stress. It's a calm momentum, fueled by clear direction and shared strength.

One of the best stories I've heard about building that kind of Intentional Resilience into a system came from Julia Anderson when she served as Global CTIO at The Campbell's Company.

When Julia arrived, she was charged with leading a large, complex technology transformation inside a legacy brand with silos, gaps in trust, and persistent cultural friction that slowed down progress.

So, she did something bold—and deceptively simple. She formed what she called the Prickly Pear Council.

Julia selected and gathered a small group of senior leaders from across the organization—people who weren't afraid to be honest and direct. Their role wasn't to sugarcoat but to surface tension: where communication was breaking down, where people were holding back, and where things felt stuck. Issues that couldn't be resolved were escalated to the Prickly Pear Council for review and resolution.

The name was part accountability, part humor. Everyone knew what it meant: This is where we talk about what's prickly before it becomes political.

Julia's plan worked. Problems started surfacing earlier, and solutions moved faster. The group became a signal that honesty was allowed and even expected.

But the real success came later, in a moment some leaders might have missed. Eventually, fewer situations were escalated, and Julia shut the council down. It had done its job. The culture had shifted. Tensions were addressed earlier in meetings. Trust was showing up in the daily rhythm. Issues were now routinely solved at the department level.

Intentional Resilience had moved from structure to reflex. And that's the goal.

When you build systems that teach people how to surface, resolve, and recover from tension early, you don't need as many interventions later. You've created anchored energy—the kind of internal culture that absorbs disruption without unraveling. That's not luck; it's Intentional Resilience by design.

The Case for Rethinking Resilience

What Julia built at Campbell's reduced friction and created space for clearer thinking, better decisions, and faster momentum. That's what Intentional Resilience does.

When Intentional Resilience isn't left to chance—when it's embedded in your systems, reinforced in your leadership, and reflected in your team's habits—it becomes more than a stress response.

It becomes an engine.

The benefits ripple across multiple layers.

Personally, you feel the difference first. There's less reactivity and more clarity. You stop spiraling in ambiguity or spinning in guilt. You recover faster from hard conversations. You hold boundaries with more ease. And you start making decisions from steadiness, not fear.

At the team level, progress starts to move forward. Meetings get more honest. Feedback becomes less personal and more productive. People stretch without snapping and recover without resentment. Retention improves and innovation increases, without external pressure. The flywheel spins more smoothly and recovers from the bumps.

At the organizational level, the transformation is even more powerful. Risk tolerance goes up. Decision fatigue goes down. Ideas rise faster, and teams self-regulate with more maturity. Leadership capacity expands beyond the executive tier because people are leading themselves well.

Intentional Resilience by design results in fewer emotional fire drills, less wasted energy, more strategic focus, and more room to grow.

During the moments that matter most—when the pressure hits, the playbook breaks, or the landscape shifts—your team won't collapse into chaos. It will stay anchored because the team members know how to move. This isn't hypothetical, it's urgent. You're building this practice into your teams now and for the future.

The Future of Intentional Resilience

We've spent time in this book exploring what Intentional Resilience looks like under pressure and how it shows up in your mindset, your systems, and your teams. But if that resilience fades away when you move on to a new role, a new team, or a new company, it was never truly embedded into the DNA of the culture. It was personality. Real Intentional Resilience—resilience that lasts—must be passed on, modeled, embedded, shared, and left as a legacy.

That's how it becomes a cultural capability, not just a personal strength dependent on the personality of a leader. To scale Intentional Resilience, it must be intentionally nurtured.

This nurturance is particularly important now because "what's coming next" isn't hypothetical, it's already here. AI is reshaping how we work, learn, and lead. Disruption is arriving faster than most systems can process. The playbooks are outdated before they're printed.

The future will demand even more of your teams: faster pivots, deeper clarity, and greater psychological range. The question isn't how resilient you are, it's whether you're building the kind of culture where Intentional Resilience is reinforced daily. You build this culture through how you lead, mentor, hire, and learn.

No one sustains Intentional Resilience in isolation, and no one learns it just by being told. Instead, people learn it by seeing it, by feeling safe enough to try and fail, and by observing how you move through the moments that matter most.

I want to close this chapter with the story of someone who's spent his life living and teaching resilience as a way of shaping what comes next.

JGo's Choice

Jason "JGo" Gordon didn't grow up with safety or stability, and he didn't even grow up with his name.

Adopted shortly after birth and renamed three times by age ten, he was raised in an environment that left him physically and emotionally unsafe. JGo learned early what many adults spend years avoiding: the truth that life can be chaotic, unfair, and isolating.

JGo learned that resilience is a choice. He made that choice around age ten. He was alone in his room, crying after yet another traumatic moment, and something in him snapped into clarity. It was his resolve. "I remember thinking, 'I'm going to get through this. And I'm going to help other kids get through their stuff, too.'"

It was a promise to himself, a personal line in the sand that shaped the course of JGo's life. He grew up, healed what he could, and started doing exactly what he'd vowed to do: help others grow through hard things.

A few years ago, JGo cofounded *Written Out Loud*, a storytelling incubator that teaches kids how to collaborate creatively and tell their stories with courage. A small group of children writes and edits a book together, which is then professionally published and also made available in the school district's library. The program has published thousands of books throughout the country. He's built a program that teaches resilience through practice, not in the abstract, but in the work. Kids in JGo's incubator learn to navigate feedback, rework drafts, support one another, and finish what they start.

And they do it with joy, as JGo models and teaches. Not "get over it." Not "push through." But something more generous, practical, and enduring:

- You are not what happened to you.
- You are what you build from what happened.
- You don't have to build it alone.

JGo's story is a reminder that resilience has to be lived, observed, and passed on by continual presence, not by a training program or employee workshop.

That's where our future begins: Not with more performance, but with more modeling. Not with grit, but with grace. Not by pretending the next generation will figure it out, but by showing them how to do it well.

JGo's story reminds me of what's at stake for kids and for all of us. The world isn't getting simpler, and the next generation will inherit more complexity. They're already watching us closely.

Building a culture of Intentional Resilience is our responsibility for business outcomes and for the people who are learning how to lead by watching us.

We can't assume Intentional Resilience will trickle down. We must model it forward so it becomes part of what we teach, reward, and reinforce every day. Mentorship is essential—not as a formal program but as the daily act of helping people grow into their strengths. We can help turn pressure into power and show, not tell, how to respond when the mission keeps changing.

When I coach executives, I remind them: "You're not just solving today's problems. You're shaping tomorrow's leadership memory. Years from now, the people you lead will face their own crisis, and they'll draw from how you showed up today."

That's what it means to mentor for Intentional Resilience: You can give people the mindset and capacity they'll carry forward, long after you're gone.

The Joy of What You've Built

A quiet joy comes with knowing you've helped someone grow stronger. You've given them space and shown up with enough steadiness, clarity, and care to help them discover their strength.

This work isn't about hitting metrics or navigating chaos. It's about nurturing a quality that lasts inside someone else.

When you mentor for Intentional Resilience, you're improving performance and giving someone a way through, a model, a memory, and a moment that tells them, "You can do this."

And one day, maybe years from now, they'll be the ones doing it for someone else. They'll be the calm voice, the steady hand, and the leader who knows how to push beyond the comfort zone without breaking, and hold space without disappearing.

It will be because of how you led when they were still finding their footing. That's your legacy, your leadership, and the future of Intentional Resilience.

ANCHORED ENERGY

I mentioned at the beginning of this book, and in the stories throughout, that the hardest decision I've ever made was the decision to shut down my company. I did it to stay aligned with my values and to honor my clarity and conviction.

The cost and the fallout can't easily be described in a few pages. Simply put, I lost everything. Financially, it was ruinous. Emotionally, it was devastating. Personally, it decimated relationships that have never been rebuilt.

That kind of blistering stress took an enormous toll on my physical and mental health and lasted for years. I won't sugarcoat it: that time period was dark, difficult, and despairing.

I tell my story often, on large keynote stages to thousands of people, in Intentional Resilience workshops with enthusiastic teams, in small settings with the boards of directors and executive leadership teams of some of the world's largest companies, and on podcasts and in interviews. I share it because it is core to who I've become and how I came to understand and share the shift from Reactive Resilience to Intentional Resilience.

Without fail, after every telling, someone asks me, "Do you have any regrets?"

My answer is a clear, unwavering "no."

I would make the same decision to shut down my company today, tomorrow, the next day, and every day after that. Even knowing the astronomical costs. It taught me about my most significant competitive advantage in my life and leadership: my Intentional Resilience.

Near the beginning of my keynote about Intentional Resilience, I ask people to envision a time in their life that required resilience. I ask them to bring it into their mind, and I ask them how that time made them feel—the emotions, the stress, and the whole experience. I ask them to remember what people in their lives told them about that time: "You'll bounce back." "You'll power through." "You'll be stronger on the other side."

And then I ask my audiences to raise their hands if those "bounce back" platitudes helped solve the situation. I never see any hands. Ever.

We're so used to the traditional definition of resilience—the "bounce back," Reactive Resilience definition—that we don't stop to re-examine it or rethink it with a critical eye or to ask ourselves, "Does this still serve me?"

When I ask my keynote audiences, as I've asked you in this book, to stop and think deeply about the times you've needed to lean into resilience, a visceral realization emerges. We come to understand how terribly flawed the Reactive Resilience model is.

Earning a "badge" of resilience only after experiencing tough times is limiting. It encourages us to bounce back to normal life without building critical skills like anticipation, flexibility, and adaptability. The traditional definition of resilience no longer reflects what our world looks like.

That's why I'm so passionate about sharing this mindset shift to Intentional Resilience. This journey we've been on together—rethinking resilience from the ground up—brings clarity and builds courage. It takes the kind of leadership that doesn't wait for a crisis to prove itself, but instead, grows ahead of the curve.

Much of this book has clearly been about work and leadership. Topics like AI, decision-making, team dynamics, sharing knowledge, and setting boundaries on your calendar are all part of this. But the benefits of shifting to Intentional Resilience don't stay in your inbox or in the boardroom.

They travel with you into your home, relationships, and community. Your new understanding of Intentional Resilience influences how you parent, partner, interact, and navigate every aspect of your life.

When you build it well, you don't need to compartmentalize it. The same clarity that helps you lead a product launch also helps you navigate a hard conversation with your teenager. The same community you build at work strengthens how you show up in your neighborhood or your faith circle. The same cadence that prevents burnout in a high-growth role is what allows you to rest, reset, and be fully present in all aspects of your life.

I've seen it in my coaching clients:

- A CEO reconnecting more deeply with his kids.
- A founder learning to ask for help and finding that it made her stronger.
- A VP teaching her daughter how to "normalize the stretch" before a big audition.

Rethinking resilience isn't just leadership training, it's a life training. When you build Intentional Resilience across your ecosystems, you stop switching gears and start showing up whole to everything.

Recap: The Flywheel in Full

You've seen how Intentional Resilience works—not as a response to crisis but as a system of motion and a way of leading, deciding, and recovering with clarity and confidence across every ecosystem of your life.

Let's recap what you've built:

- **Conviction**: Anchored tenacity in the face of any opportunity or challenge.
- **Curiosity**: A posture of openness that keeps you learning.
- **Clarity**: Prioritizing what matters most, even under pressure.
- **Communication**: Transmitting trust as well as information.
- **Community**: Collective strength and mutual accountability.
- **Cadence**: A sustainable, optimal rhythm of action and decisions.

- **Capabilities**: The habits, systems, and skills that make all the rest actionable.

Together, these elements create endurance and generate energy.

Intentional Resilience by design isn't reactive. It's regenerative. And now it's yours.

Repeatable Intentional Resilience

Even when I tell people that I would make the same decision to shut down my company, there's some skepticism. So, I expand on what a positive difference this one decision made.

I found clarity in my values—and in my willingness to do the hard thing when it's the right thing, turning pressure into power.

This is my competitive advantage. And it naturally leads to other benefits.

I have nothing weighing on my shoulders, on my mind, or on my heart.

I'm anchored by my values and energized by my Intentional Resilience.

My experience was a gift. Nothing happened *to* me. Everything happens *through* me. Intentionally.

The clarity, the confidence, and the energy it gave me in my soul could not have been achieved any other way. And that's why I share this powerful shift with you: the powerful shift from Reactive Resilience to Intentional Resilience.

The most powerful step is to start, to recognize that you already *have* resilience, and to strengthen it intentionally so you can thrive.

And, one of the most exciting parts of Intentional Resilience is that it's not a finite resource. The more you tap into it, the more it becomes available whenever you need it. And when you have more resilience, you can share it with all the people who matter—your family, your team, and your friends.

So, let's wrap up with a challenge:

Try to implement the Intentional Resilience flywheel into your work and your life. And remember the three habits I mentioned to you way back in Chapter 2, the habits I call the "3 R's": Reflect, Repeat, and Replace.

I'll run through them one more time for you.

- **Reflect.** Take a moment to pause. Give yourself space to gain clarity on what's truly important, such as your values and priorities. When others are confused, you'll have clarity and conviction.
- **Repeat.** Build those reflections into micro-moments and practice them regularly. When others hesitate, you'll have the confidence of muscle memory.
- **Replace.** Transform your Reactive Resilience into Intentional Resilience. When others are constrained and unsure, you'll be energized by the shift.

On the first page of the Introduction, I told you about a competitive advantage you probably didn't know about. Now that you do, all you need to do is **choose it.**

So, don't believe the dictionary definition of resilience: You don't need to bounce back if you're unshakable from the start. When you rethink resilience, you can choose Intentional Resilience.

Instead of things happening *to you,* you *choose* what happens *through you*: growth, curiosity, exploration, and innovation. You gain clarity and confidence, anchored in your values. This knowledge gives you energy— the fuel to do what truly matters.

This is your competitive advantage *and* your legacy.

You will be successful, anchored, and fulfilled. And you will thrive.

I can't wait to see what you do next.

So … what are you waiting for?

Be Intentional

I wrote *Rethinking Resilience* to spark a shift—from bouncing back to building strength by design. At www.tissarichards.com, you'll find tools, guides, and practices to help you carry this shift forward in your own leadership and life.

Share Your Experience

If these ideas resonated with you, I'd love for you to leave a review. Your words not only help others discover the book, they help grow a community of Intentionally Resilient leaders.

ACKNOWLEDGMENTS

We had a creative program in my elementary school library. Kids wrote short stories and typed them up, and volunteers "bound" them into books using donated wallpaper. (This being the 1990s, the wallpaper was interesting, by today's design standards. It was loud, colorful, and full of patterns and swirls.)

I was a prolific young author in this program. And every book of mine was dedicated to my parents, my dogs, and my favorite teachers.

Little did I know that, decades later, my second book would be published "for real." That the work of designing a cover would be much harder than choosing from leftover donated wallpaper. That the writing would take more than one to two days of an elementary creative writing class. And, that the Acknowledgments page would be filled with many more people than in the dedications of those early literary attempts.

But it is a reality that writing a real, grown-up book takes an actual village. And I am eternally grateful to that village—so, let's dive in.

To my mother, who is my rock. I love you.

To the Benets and Zwahlens—my chosen family, I could not have come through the last years without your love and support. I love you, and I'm so grateful to you. To the Wilkinsons and Murpheys—my "extra" sets of parents (and Queenie and Blackjack, who kept me company while I brainstormed in your living room)—thank you, and I love you.

In tribute to Lorraine Hendrickson. You are a beam of light, a joy, and a fierce example of Intentional Resilience. (I refuse to use the word "were" because you will always be these things.) I am honored to be your friend and will miss you always.

Joanna Furlong, Ally Zwahlen, and Cali Ressler—readers, friends, and sounding boards. Thank you for always answering the "ping, ping, ping" of my texts and my incessant emails with questions. You helped shape this book.

Shar Kassam, you kicked off this journey when the days were dark and I had no idea what was around the next corner. I am forever grateful to you and for you.

Mr. James Albery, you helped me find my voice so long ago. I wish you were here to see it soar.

A behind-the-scenes team makes a book possible and seem so effortless. Ripple Impact, Lynne Klippel, Mike Colapietro, Anne Janzer, Carla Green, Jennifer Jas, and my launch team. Without you, this would still be an idea in my head and in my heart.

Jon Meadows, thank you for the beautiful back cover photo (and all the other photos).

To my HPS24 Wicked Cohort, your generosity and time in crafting the keynote that goes with this book is immeasurable and appreciated.

Grace Migliaccio and John Hiron, you opened your home and your hearts as I kept coming back (and back, and back) to perfect a craft. I'm so honored to call you friends. And to Diane Honda—I'm so grateful you introduced us.

To the contributors who shared their stories in this book—thank you for your remarkable stories, insights, and vulnerability. Your generosity made this a far more enjoyable read than my voice alone would have been.

To the Empowerment Collective—all of you—you fill up my cup, and I appreciate each of you.

And, to the people who inspired this book. The brave leaders and founders, the remarkable humans I know and have had the immense privilege of working with and observing in action. Without you, I wouldn't understand what resilience truly is, how to build it, and how to teach it to others.

ABOUT THE AUTHOR

Tissa Richards is a leadership expert, keynote speaker, and award-winning author on a mission to help bold, high-capacity leaders become unshakable.

She works with leaders and teams who are done with burnout, noise, and over-performing—and are ready to lead with clarity, confidence, and zero compromise. Her work helps them make high-stakes decisions without losing themselves, communicate with credibility, and turn pressure into power.

A repeat tech founder and CEO, Tissa has built and led companies from the ground up, raised millions in funding, and holds multiple patents for enterprise cybersecurity software. She now advises Fortune 500 companies, high-growth startups, and private equity-backed firms, helping leadership teams drive innovation, performance, and outcomes—without compromising who they are.

Tissa's first book, *No Permission Needed*, is a five-time award winner and Amazon bestseller.

Learn more at tissarichards.com or connect on LinkedIn.